ILLUSTRATED ENCYCLOPEDIA

CLASSIC DAYS
OF STEAM

ILLUSTRATED ENCYCLOPEDIA

CLASSIC DAYS OF STEAM

COLIN GARRATT

LORENZ BOOKS

ACKNOWLEDGMENTS

The Publishers would like to thank the following for their kind permission to reproduce photographs in this book:

A. E. Durrant: pages 36 (bl), 38 (br).
Howard Ande: page 4.
British Waterways Archive: page 8 (t).
Colour Rail: page 64 (b).
Roger Crombleholme: pages 15 (t,b), 16, 17 (b), 18 (t,b), 19 (b).
Richard Gruber: pages 75 (t), 76 (b).
Alex Grunbach: pages 48, 49 (t,b), 116, 117.
John P. Hankey: pages 22 (t,m), 23 (t), 26 (t), 27 (m), 28 (top), 30 (b), 32 (t), 33 (b), 72 (b), 73 (t), 74 (t), 75 (m), 77 (m), 83 (t), 85 (t).
Michael Hinckley: page 15 (m).
Fred Hornby: pages 104 (t), 106 (br), 107 (t), 108, 109.

Locomotive Manufacturer's Association: page 67 (br).
Dennis Lovett: page 14 (b).
Arthur Mace: pages 10 (b), 13 (tr), 63 (t,b).
William D. Middleton Collection: pages 44 (b), 45 (t,b).
Mitchel Library: pages 29 (b), 33 (t,m), 39 (br), 44 (t), 45 (m), 47 (t), 49 (m), 50 (m), 52–3, 115 (t), 119 (m), 122 (b).
Alan Pike: pages 37 (b), 50 (t), 98, 99 (b), 100 (b), 101 (b), 102, 103.
Graham Pike: pages 105 (l).
Popperfoto: pages 23 (m), 29 (m), 32 (b), 35, 36 (br), 47 (b), 54 (t,b), 92 (m), 93 (m), 121 (tr).
William Sharman: pages 58 (b), 59 (t), 68 (b) 69 (t).
Brian Solomon: pages 23 (b), 24 (t,b), 28 (m,b), 30 (t), 31 (m,b), 70, 71 (m,b), 72 (t), 73 (m), 74 (b),

76 (t), 80 (t), 84 (b), 85 (m,b), 87 (b).
Richard J. Solomon: pages 71 (t), 73 (b), 77 (b), 80 (b), 82, 83 (b), 84 (t), 86 (t, br), 87 (t,m), 88, 89 (t,m), 90 (top), 91, 92 (t,b), 93 (t,b).
Gordon Stemp: pages 58 (t), 61 (b), 64 (b), 81 (t).
J. M. Tolson: page 104 (b).
Verkehrsmuseums Nürnberg: pages 36 (t), 37 (t).
Max Wade-Matthews: page 8 (b).
Neil Wheelwright: page 106 (bl).
Ron Ziel: pages 26 (t), 77 (t), 81 (b), 90 (b), 115 (br)

All other pictures courtesy of **Milepost 92^1/2**.

t=top, b=bottom, l=left, r=right, m=middle.

This edition first published by Lorenz Books
an imprint of Anness Publishing Limited
Hermes House, 88–89 Blackfriars Road, London, SE1 8HA

Published in the USA by Lorenz Books
Anness Publishing Inc., 27 West 20th Street, New York, NY 10011; (800) 354-9657

© 1998, 2000 Anness Publishing Limited

This edition distributed in Canada by Raincoast Books
8680 Cambie Street, Vancouver, British Columbia, V6P 6M9

A CIP catalogue record for this book is available from the British Library

Publisher Joanna Lorenz
Editorial Manager Helen Sudell
Assistant Editor Emma Gray
Designer Michael Morey

Previously published as *The Golden Age of Steam*

This book has been written and picture researched by the Milepost Publishing Production Team: Milepost also conserves and markets collections of railway transparencies and negatives. Milepost 92^1/2, Newton Harcourt, Leicestershire LE8 9FH

For historical reasons, the measurements in this book are not always given with their metric or imperial equivalent. See page 128 for a conversion chart.

Printed and bound in Hong Kong
1 3 5 7 9 10 8 6 4 2

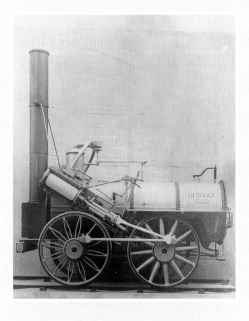

CONTENTS

The Birth of the Railway

The following section looks at the development of the railway, from its very beginnings up to 1900, touching on both the technical changes it underwent and the role it played in societies and industries around the world. The text and photographs provide a comprehensive account of the railway pioneers and the machines and lines they created, while the technical boxes give an at-a-glance record of some of the most influential and innovative locomotives.

● **OPPOSITE**
Locomotion No. 1 – a working replica built in 1975. The first locomotive built at the Stephensons' Forth Street works, Newcastle upon Tyne, in 1825, it also established the advent of mechanical traction for public railways. The original locomotive survives in Darlington Railway Museum, County Durham, north-east England.

● **ABOVE**
A Puffing Billy-type engine built by William Hedley of Wylam Colliery, Northumberland, in 1813. From a painting by David Weston (born 1936).

FROM TRAMWAYS
TO STEAM

In Britain, one of the first tramways was
built about 1630 to serve collieries near
Newcastle upon Tyne. The Tanfield
Waggonway in County Durham was
begun about 1725, and by 1727 included
the Causey Arch, the world's first railway
viaduct, built by Ralph Wood. At first,
the rails were made of wood but these
wore quickly, and in 1767 iron plates
were affixed to them for durability. The
first cast-iron plates were made by the
Coalbrookdale Ironworks in Shropshire.
Plate rails, that is iron-flanged rails, were
introduced underground at Sheffield Park
Colliery in 1787 and on the surface at
Ketley Incline in 1788.

● STAGECOACH IMPROVES ROADS

Transportation in the 17th and 18th
centuries was either by stagecoach or
water. In 1658, the state of the roads was
so bad that the stagecoach took two
weeks to travel from London to
Edinburgh. Even by the end of the
1700s, with responsibility for the
maintenance of main roads handed from
parishes to turnpike trusts, the state of
the roads was not much better. In winter,
they were blocked by snow or floods; in

summer, hard-baked ruts made journeys
uncomfortable. This was acceptable while
most travel was on horseback. With the
ever-increasing use of coaches for public
transport, however, the roads improved.
By the 1750s the stagecoach had come
into its own.

● RAILWAYS REPLACE WATERWAYS

With industrialization, however, the need
for transportation of heavy goods
remained. By about the mid-18th
century, artificial canals came into being

as arteries for goods making their way to
the larger rivers and to the sea for export
to various parts of Britain. The
waterways' half-century of posterity and
public service ended, however, with the
coming of the railways. Many became
ruins or were bought by local railway
companies. Turnpike roads ceased to be
the chief arteries of the nation's
lifeblood. Posting-inns were replaced by
hotels springing up at railway termini.
The Railway Era saw the demise of the
public mailcoach and heavy family coach.
In some instances, however, when such
conservative-minded gentry as the Duke
of Wellington travelled by rail, they sat in
their coaches, which were placed on flat
trucks. By 1840, with railways halving the
cost of travel, canal and stagecoach were
doomed.

● THE FIRST RAILWAYS

In 1804, the world's first public
railway company, the Surrey Iron
Railway Company, opened a horse-drawn
line from Wandsworth Wharf, on the
River Thames in south London, to
Croydon in Surrey. The line was
extended to Merstham, Surrey, but

This historic event saw the world's first
public railway regularly to use steam
locomotives to haul wagons of goods (the
main traffic was coal) and carriages of
passengers. Passengers were carried in
horse-drawn coaches until 1833.

In 1829, Lancashire's Liverpool &
Manchester Railway, built mainly to carry
cotton, offered a £500 prize to the
winner of a competition for the best
steam-locomotive design to work the line.
The trials were held at Rainhill, near
Liverpool. Of the three locomotives
entered, George Stephenson's Rocket,
gaily painted yellow, black and white, won
at a speed of about 26 mph (42 kph).

never reached its intended destination,
Portsmouth in Hampshire.

● RICHARD TREVITHICK

Another landmark in the history of
railways also occurred in 1804 when
British engineer Richard Trevithick
(1771–1833) tested his newly invented
steam locomotive. This drew five wagons
and a coach with 70 passengers along the
ten miles of track from the Pen-y-Darren
Ironworks to the Glamorganshire Canal.
This historic event saw the world's first
steam locomotive to run on rails hauling
a train carrying fare-paying passengers.

Trevithick continued his experiments
and in 1808 erected a circular track in
Euston Square, London, on which he ran
his latest production "Catch Me Who
Can". The public was invited to pay a
shilling, almost a day's wages for the
average working man, to ride on this

novel method of transportation, but the
venture failed financially and in a few
weeks Trevithick had to close it.

● GEORGE STEPHENSON

Between 1814–21 Northumbrian
engineer George Stephenson (1781–
1848), born in Wylam, a village near
Newcastle upon Tyne, built 17
experimental locomotives. Although he
was not the first to produce a steam
locomotive, he was the prime mover in
introducing them on a wide scale. His
turning-point came in 1821 when he was
appointed engineer-in-charge of what
became the 42 km (26 mile) long
Stockton & Darlington Railway, between
the County Durham towns of Stockton-
on-Tees, a seaport, and Darlington, an
industrial centre. It was opened in
September 1825. Stephenson's
Locomotion No. 1 drew the first train.

ROCKET

Date	1829
Builder	George Stephenson
Client	Liverpool &
Manchester Railway
(L&MR)
Gauge	4 ft 8½ in
Type	0-2-2
Capacity	2 cylinders outside
8 x 17 in inclined
Pressure	50 lb
Weight	4 tons 5 cwt

BRITISH LOCOMOTIVES OF THE 1830s

By 1830 almost 100 locomotives had been built in Britain. These early experimental engines were of two main types: those with inclined cylinders and those with vertical cylinders. Then, in 1830 George Stephenson introduced the 2-2-0 Planet type. This was a radical step forward from the Rocket and its derivatives and established the general form that all future steam locomotives were to take. Planet combined the multi-tubular boiler with a fully water-jacketed firebox and a separate smokebox. The cylinders were now inside and horizontally mounted, while the engine's boiler and motion were carried on a sturdy outside frame of oak beams sandwiched by iron plates. The first Planet was a passenger-engine with 5 ft driving wheels and 3 ft carrying wheels, but Stephenson was quick to see that the frame arrangement would allow him to substitute two pairs of coupled 4 ft 6 in wheels to create a heavy-goods locomotive. The resulting engines, Samson and Goliath, were supplied to the Liverpool & Manchester Railway (L&MR) in 1831.

● **ABOVE**
Robert Stephenson (1803–59): at the age of 20 he was put in charge of his father's locomotive works in Newcastle upon Tyne. He became the leading locomotive engineer of his day. He built railway bridges and viaducts, notably the tubular bridge over the Menai Strait between Anglesey and mainland Wales.

● **BELOW**
Lion, built in the same year as Samson, shows how far heavy-goods engine design had really progressed. The first engine built by Todd, Kitson & Laird, this 0-4-2 had 5 ft driving wheels and is still in working order.

PATENTEE	
Date	1833
Builder	Robert Stephenson
Client	Liverpool & Manchester Railway (L&MR)
Gauge	4 ft 8^1/$_2$ in
Type	2-2-2
Driving wheels	5 ft
Capacity	2 cylinders 12 x 18 in
Pressure	50 lb

Hackworth, meanwhile, was still firmly wedded to the archaic vertical cylinder arrangement. In 1831 he built six engines of the Majestic class for heavy-coal haulage on the Stockton & Darlington Railway (S&DR). Their cylinders were carried on an overhanging platform at the back of the boiler and drove a crankshaft carried on a bracket below. The crankshaft in turn drove the nearest pair of the six coupled wheels, allowing all axles to be sprung. The boilers combined Hackworth's longitudinal flue with a return multi-tubular arrangement intended to provide the best features of both layouts. In the event, the small grate area possible in the single flue severely limited the engines' steaming power. Also, they were heavy on fuel as well as being cumbersome in appearance with a tender at each end of the locomotive. Their ponderous performance in traffic was such that the line's rigid speed limit of 6 mph (9.7 kph) did not trouble them.

Edward Bury had intended his first locomotive, Liverpool, to take part in the Rainhill Trials but it was not ready in time. Noting Rocket's superior features,

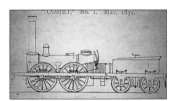

"COMET," No. 1. MAY, 1832.

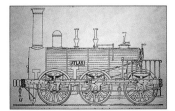

ATLAS

- **FAR LEFT**
George Stephenson (1781–1848): the world's most well-known locomotive engineer. He worked as an engineer for several railway companies and built the first railway line to carry passengers (1825).

- **ABOVE LEFT**
Comet was the first locomotive put into service on the Leicester & Swannington Railway (L&SR). On the inaugural run, in May 1832, the 13 ft high chimney was knocked down in the Glenfield Tunnel, near Leicester, covering the travelling dignitaries in soot. Swannington, in Leicestershire, is 19 km (12 miles) north-west of the county town.

- **BELOW LEFT**
Atlas was the first 0-6-0 goods engine built by Robert Stephenson. It was delivered to the L&SR in 1834. At the time, this was the largest, heaviest and most powerful locomotive running on any railway.

he was able to modify his design and deliver the engine to the L&MR in 1830. In its rebuilt form, it was bristling with innovations and became an international prototype. Most striking were the 6 ft coupled wheels, bigger than any previously made, but equally notable were the multi-tubular boiler, inside bar-frames and raised-dome firebox-casing. The cylinders, too, were inside, inclined slightly upwards to allow the piston rods to pass beneath the leading axle. On the line, Liverpool proved capable of hauling an 18-wagon train at an average of 12^1/$_2$ mph (19 kph). In short, she was a stunning little creation, topped off by a small chimney with a procession of

cutout brass liver birds around its crown. (The liver is a fanciful bird on the arms of the city of Liverpool.)

With progress came the need for more powerful locomotives, and it had to be admitted that Planets were unsteady at any speed and their firebox capacity was limited. Robert Stephenson rectified this by extending the frames rearwards, adding a trailing axle behind a much-enlarged firebox. Thus was born the Patentee 2-2-2 Type, which became the standard British express-engine for the next four decades and was exported widely to inaugurate railway services across Europe. Stephenson's Patentees also incorporated great improvements in

boiler construction and valve gear. All had flangeless driving wheels.

The design could be varied to incorporate coupled driving wheels, as other manufacturers were quick to see. Perhaps the best known front-coupled Patentee is the 0-4-2 Lion, built for the L&MR in 1838 by Todd, Kitson & Laird of Leeds, Yorkshire.

- **BELOW**
Samson, built by Timothy Hackworth in 1838 for heavy-goods work on the Stockton & Darlington Railway (S&DR), already looked outdated by the standards of the time. Note the fireman feeding the single-flue boiler from the front end.

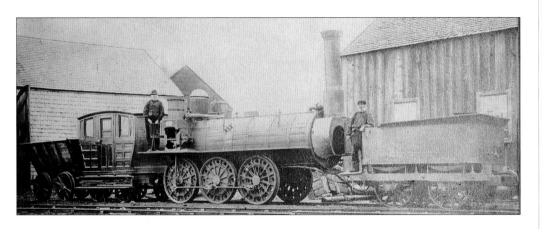

THE BATTLE OF THE GAUGES

Isambard Kingdom Brunel (1806–59) conceived railways on a grand scale. For his Great Western Railway (GWR), authorized in 1835, he dismissed the well-established 4 ft 8½ in gauge as inadequate to cope with the greater speeds, safety and smoother travel he planned for his relatively straight and level main line from London to Bristol. So he fixed his gauge at a spacious 7 ft. The main drawbacks were that this set the GWR apart from all other railways and meant that all goods and passengers had to change trains when travelling to or from areas not served by GWR trains.

The first GWR train steamed out of Paddington Station, west London, on 4 June 1838 behind the Stephenson 2-2-2 North Star, a large example of the Patentee type, which was originally built for the 5 ft 6 in gauge New Orleans Railway in the USA. A broken contract caused her to be altered to 7 ft gauge and to go to the GWR instead. A sister engine, Morning Star, entered service at the same time. North Star had 7 ft driving wheels and the inside-cylinders

● LEFT
A classic GWR broad-gauge single powers an express-train westwards through the Sonning Cutting, near Reading, Berkshire. It is late in the broad-gauge era for a third rail has been laid on each track to allow rolling stock of both gauges to operate.

were 16 x 16 in. Obsolescence was rapid in those days, but North Star was rebuilt with a large boiler and new cylinders in 1854, lasting in service for 33 years. When finally withdrawn, she was preserved at Swindon, Wiltshire, until, in an act of official vandalism, she was scrapped in 1906. In something of an atonement, GWR built a full-sized replica incorporating original parts in 1925. This is displayed at Swindon Railway Museum.

For the most part, the other original GWR broad-gauge locomotives were a collection of mechanical freaks, the best of a poor lot being six 2-2-2s with 8 ft driving wheels from Tayleur's Vulcan Foundry, which were Patentee copies but

IRON DUKE	
Date	1847
Builder	Daniel Gooch, Swindon, Wiltshire, England
Client	Great Western Railway (GWR)
Gauge	7 ft
Type	4-2-2
Driving wheels	8 ft
Capacity	2 cylinders 18 x 24 in
Pressure	100 lb later 120 lb
Weight	35 tons

● **ABOVE LEFT**
The importance of the broad gauge and its
hitherto unimagined speeds caught the
imagination of the populace. People flocked to
experience this revolutionary form of travel in
which speeds of 90 mph (145 kph) had been
reported.

● **ABOVE RIGHT**
Tiny: built by Sara & Co., of Plymouth, Devon,
in 1868, this broad-gauge locomotive went
into service on England's South Devon
Railway (SDR).

● **OPPOSITE MIDDLE**
Isambard Kingdom Brunel (1806–59), the
19th-century English engineer who pioneered
the broad gauge of the Great Western Railways,
between London and Exeter in Devon. His
father was a French engineer in England, Sir
Marc Isambard Brunel (1769–1849).

● **OPPOSITE BOTTOM**
Iron Duke (replica): built by Gooch, this 4-2-2
of the Duke Class was named after Arthur
Wellesley, the first Duke of Wellington
(1769–1852), on whose birthday – 1 May – it
first ran.

with small low-pressure boilers. They
were delivered from Manchester,
Lancashire, to London by sea and then
on to West Drayton, Middlesex, by canal.
Among their more bizarre stablemates
were two 2-2-2s from Mather & Dixon
with 10 ft driving wheels fabricated from
riveted iron plates.

There was much opposition to the
broad gauge, and in July 1845 the Gauge
Commission sat to choose between the
rival claims of both gauges. High-speed
trial runs were organized, the honours
going to Daniel Gooch's 7 ft GWR single
"Ixion", which achieved 60 mph (96.6

kph) hauling an 80 ton (81,284 kg) train.
The best standard-gauge performance was
53 mph (85.1 kph) behind a brand new
Stephenson 4-2-0 with 6 ft 6 in driving
wheels. Although the Commission
considered the 7 ft gauge in every way
superior, the standard gauge was selected
on the basis of the greater mileage
already in use. In 1848, Parliament
decided there should in future be only
one gauge, the narrow, and eventually the
GWR had to bow to the inevitable, laying
a third rail to give 4 ft 8½ in throughout
its system and abolishing the broad gauge
altogether in May 1892.

● **RIGHT**
Rain, Steam and Speed (National Gallery,
London): Turner (1775–1851), the English
landscape painter, welcomed the Industrial
Revolution of the 18th and 19th centuries and
painted this picture of one of Gooch's singles
crossing the Maidenhead Viaduct, Berkshire,
during a squally storm in the Thames valley.

BRITISH LOCOMOTIVES – 1840–60

● BELOW
Derwent: built by W.A. Kitching in 1845, this 0-6-0 went into service on the Stockton & Darlington Railway (S&DR) between Stockton-on-Tees port and Darlington, County Durham, the first passenger-carrying railway in the world (1825). This railway largely developed the industrial town.

In 1841, Robert Stephenson introduced the first of his "long-boilered" locomotives. In these, he sought to obtain greater boiler power by grouping all the axles in front of the firebox and having a much longer boiler barrel than usual. The necessarily short wheelbase was dictated by the small turntables of the period. "Long-boiler" engines also featured inside frames of iron-plate and the inside-cylinders shared a common steam-chest placed between them. The design could be built in almost any form: a 2-2-2 or 2-4-0 for passenger work and an 0-6-0 for goods-trains were the commonest configurations. But as line speeds rose, the passenger types were found to oscillate dangerously on their short wheelbase chassis and soon fell out of favour. For goods work, however, the design was an undoubted success and these were most numerous on Stephenson's home turf. The North Eastern Railway (NER), a successor to the Stockton & Darlington Railway (S&DR), had no fewer than 125 long-boiler 0-6-0s of the 1001 class built between 1852 and 1875. Fittingly, No. 1275 is preserved in the National Railway Museum at York.

Thomas Russell Crampton (1816–88) was an ambitious young engineer working at Swindon, Wiltshire, under Daniel Gooch. He began to develop his own ideas for an express-locomotive with a large boiler and driving wheels but low centre of gravity and took out his first patent in 1842. In his design, the driving axle was placed right at the base of the frame, behind the firebox. To keep the connecting-rods as short as possible, the cylinders were displaced rearwards outside the frames and fed from the smokebox by prominent outside steam-pipes. The motion and valve gear was all placed outside, allowing the boiler to

LARGE BLOOMER	
Date	1852
Builder	W. Fairbairn/ E.B. Wilson
Client	London & North Western Railway (LNWR)
Gauge	4 ft 8 1/2 in
Type	2-2-2
Driving wheels	7 ft 6 in
Capacity	2 cylinders 18 x 24 in
Pressure	150 lb
Weight	31 tons 4 cwt

● BELOW MIDDLE
A 2-2-2 Single of 1851 built by Robert
Stephenson for LNWR.

● BELOW
The classic outline of E.B. Wilson's Jenny Lind
as painted by architect and Royal Academy
summer exhibitor Ernest W. Twining.

be sunk down in the frames but making
the engine very wide. Crampton left the
GWR to promote his design to a wider
market. His first two engines were built
by Tulk & Ley for the Liège & Namur
Railway, Belgium, in 1846.

One of the Cramptons destined for
Belgium was tested on the Grand
Junction Railway (GJR), leading the
London and North Western Railway
(LNWR) to build one for themselves at
Crewe, Cheshire, in 1847. This was the
4-2-0 Courier with 7 in driving wheels,
inside-frames and a boiler of oval cross-
section. At the same time, larger versions
with 8 in driving wheels, the 4-2-0
London by Tulk & Ley and the 6-2-0
Liverpool by Bury, Curtis & Kennedy,
were tried out by the LNWR, the latter
with great destructive effect on the track.
Cramptons could run at speeds
approaching 90 mph (145 kph), but they
never achieved great popularity in Britain
because of their rough riding caused by
the position of the driving axle. On the
Continent, it was a different matter and
the French Northern Railway in
particular gained its reputation for
lightweight fast expresses by the use of
Crampton locomotives. "Prendre le
Crampton" even entered the French

language as slang for "a quick getaway".
These French Cramptons had very strong
outside-frames, because the continental
loading-gauge left room for the resulting
enormous width over cylinders and
cranks. A British example built the same

way by J.E. McConnell of LNWR earned
the nickname "Mac's Mangle" following
the trail of broken platforms and lineside
structures left in its wake.

In 1847, from E.B. Wilson's Railway
Foundry in Leeds, Yorkshire, emerged
the first engine built to their most
famous design, the Jenny Lind class. This
2-2-2 passenger-engine was the
brainchild of the young chief
draughtsman, David Joy. Built at a cost of
about £2,500 each, the basic model had
6 in driving wheels powered by
15 x 20 in inside-cylinders, making it
capable of a mile-a-minute in regular
service. For the first time, railways could
buy an off-the-peg express locomotive of
peerless quality. This most elegant
machine, with its polished mahogany
boiler lagging and classically fluted bronze
dome and safety-valve casings, rapidly
became top-link motive power for many
of Britain's main lines. The largest Jenny
Lind was the Salopian built for
Shrewsbury & Birmingham Railway
(S&BR) in June 1849. It had a boiler
with more than 1,270 sq ft of heating
surface and a pressure of 120 lb
with 15½ x 22 in cylinders driving
6 ft 6 in wheels.

● OPPOSITE
Built by W. Fairbairn
and E.B. Wilson for
the LNWR, this Large
Bloomer is pictured at
Milton Keynes Central
in 1992. The English
new town in Bucking-
hamshire was founded
in 1967.

● RIGHT
The inside-framed
Crampton Kinnaird,
built for Scotland's
Dundee & Perth
Junction Railway by
Tulk & Ley in 1848.

BRITISH LOCOMOTIVES – 1860–75

Patrick Stirling's early locomotives were cabless and had domed boilers. His first 2-2-2 was built for Scotland's Glasgow & South Western Railway (G&SWR) in 1857 and bore many of the design hallmarks that were refined into their finest flowering in his Great Northern 4-2-2 No. 1 of 1870. His crowning achievements were the 8 ft 4-2-2 singles, built at Doncaster, Yorkshire, from 1870 onwards, said to be one of the most handsome locomotives ever made. With modification these were used on all mainline trains for the next 25 years. In 1895, they took part in the railway Races to the North with average speeds of more than 80 mph (129 kph) between King's Cross Station, London, and York.

When William Stroudley became Locomotive Superintendent of the London, Brighton & South Coast Railway (LB&SCR) in 1870, he found a bizarre assortment of locomotives, which were

by no means a match for the work they had to do. Over the next two decades, he restocked with a fine series of soundly engineered machines for every purpose from express-passenger to branch-line

haulage. His smallest, yet most celebrated class, was the Terrier 0-6-0Ts of 1872. Fifty engines were built, originally for suburban work in south London but later widely dispersed to more rural

● ABOVE
William Stroudley's beautiful livery is captured to perfection on Terrier 0-6-0T No. 55 Stepney, built in 1875 and preserved in full working order on England's Bluebell Railway in Sussex.

● LEFT
Kirtley's double-framed 2-4-0 No. 158A breathes the spirit of the Midland Railway in the 19th century at the Midland Railway Centre, Butterley, Derbyshire. Butterley was a seat of ironworks and collieries.

A 4-2-2 Massey Bromley of 1879. Dübs & Co. built ten for the Great Eastern Railway (GER). Kitsons built ten more in 1881–2.

A 2-4-0 of Scotland's Highland Railway in about 1877. Note the louvred chimney, which produced a current of air with the object of lifting the exhaust above the cab.

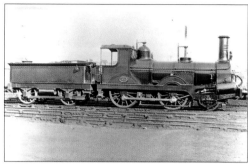

surroundings. They had 4 ft driving wheels, a 150 lb boiler and 12 x 20 in cylinders. Most were rebuilt with slightly larger boilers without in any way spoiling their appearance. Always useful, they notched up a working life of more than 90 years. Today, nearly a dozen exist in preservation.

Joseph Beattie of the London & South Western Railway (L&SWR) was an ingenious Irishman who sought to increase the steaming power of the locomotive boiler by incorporating elaborate firebox arrangements. A typical Beattie firebox had two compartments, divided by a water-filled partition. Heavy firing took place in the rear portion, the forward fire being kept as far as possible in an incandescent state. Like Kirtley, he made great use of the 2-4-0 type, both in tender form as an express-engine and as a tank-engine for suburban work. He was determined to obtain the maximum steam output from every ounce of coal, and his express 2-4-0s also featured combustion chambers, thermic siphons and auxiliary chimneys. His 2-4-0 tank-engines carried their water supply in a well-tank between the frames. In 1874, 88 entered service.

Joseph Beattie's L&SWR express 2-4-0 Medusa, fitted with double firebox and auxiliary chimney, as captured by artist Cuthbert Hamilton Ellis (born 1909).

STIRLING SINGLE	
Date	1870
Builder	Doncaster, Yorkshire, England
Client	Great Northern Railway (GNR)
Gauge	4 ft 8 1/2 in
Type	2-4-0
Driving wheels	8 ft 1 in
Capacity	2 cylinders 18 x 28 in outside
Pressure	140 lb
Weight	38 tons 9 cwt

BRITISH LOCOMOTIVES – 1875–1900

In 1882 Francis William Webb designed a three-cylinder compound express-engine with uncoupled driving wheels – the 2-2-2-0. The engine, LNWR No. 66 Experiment, had two outside high-pressure cylinders driving the rear axle and one huge low-pressure cylinder between the frames driving the leading axle. The absence of coupling-rods meant that one pair of wheels could slip without the other, and it was not unknown for the driving wheels to revolve in opposite directions when attempts were made to start the train. The best of this type were the Teutonics introduced in 1889, with their larger boilers and 7 ft 1 in driving wheels.

The first main-line 0-8-0 tender-engine to run in Britain was introduced on the newly opened Barry Railway in 1889. Built by Sharp, Stewart of Glasgow, they proved ideal for hauling heavy South Wales coal-trains, with their 18 x 26 in outside-cylinders and 4 ft-3 in driving wheels.

● **ABOVE**
The Jones Goods engines of 1894 were Britain's first 4-6-0s. No. 103 shows off its immaculate Highland Railway livery and Jones's louvred chimney.

● **ABOVE**
F.W. Webb's LNWR Precedent 2-4-0s were introduced in 1874. By 1882, the Crewe works had built 90 examples. They performed prodigious feats of haulage, culminating in No. 790 Hardwicke's performance in the 1895 Race to the North. Although Webb tried to displace them from top-link work with his compounds, the little 2-4-0s were the most reliable of all 19th-century LNWR passenger types.

● **LEFT**
A Neilson & Co. 4-2-2 with 7 ft driving wheels. Built in 1886, it is seen here in 1963, before heading the Blue Belle excursion.

● **OPPOSITE**
This Johnson Single of the former Midland Railway is one of a class known as Spinners, regarded by many as the most beautiful locomotives of all time. With variations, the class totalled 95 engines, all in service by 1900.

● **ABOVE LEFT**
Ivatt's Great Northern No. 990 was the first British Atlantic 4-4-2 and was built at Doncaster Works, Yorkshire, in 1898. Ten more were in service by 1900. In 1902, a larger boiler version appeared, No. 251, which was the first of one of Britain's most successful express-passenger types. Both the original engines are preserved and are shown here running together.

● **ABOVE RIGHT**
Nicknamed Cauliflowers because of the appearance of the LNWR coat of arms on their driving splashers resembling that vegetable, these were F.W. Webb's 18 in express goods-engines, 310 of which were built between 1880 and the turn of the century.

A serious problem on many railways was the blowing back of the exhaust into the crew's faces as they descended gradients. To remedy this, in 1877 David Jones of the Highland Railway introduced locomotives with a louvred chimney. This produced a current of air that lifted the exhaust above the cab. Jones also introduced a counter-pressure brake to assist in controlling trains descending the formidable Highland gradients. His most famous locomotives were his 4-6-0s of 1894, the first engines of this wheel arrangement to work in the British Isles. Sharp, Stewart built 15, which were, at the time, the most powerful main-line engines in Britain.

Few inside-cylinder 4-4-0s surpassed Dugald Drummond's famed T9s of 1899 for the London & South Western Railway (L&SWR). By extending the coupled wheelbase of his earlier designs to 10 ft, he made room in his T9s for a large firebox. The new engines were a success. With their 6 ft 7 in driving wheels, they were fast and able to haul heavy expresses over the difficult South Western main line west of Salisbury, Wiltshire.

CAULIFLOWER

Date	1880
Builder	F.W. Webb, Crewe Works, Cheshire, England
Client	London & North Western Railway (LNWR)
Gauge	4 ft 8^1/$_2$ in
Type	0-6-0
Driving wheels	5 ft 2 in
Capacity	Cylinders 18 in x 24 in
Pressure	150 lb
Weight	36 tons

BRITISH BUILDERS OF THE 19TH CENTURY

Britain's railways were developed piecemeal by private companies with locomotives coming from outside firms, but once the operating companies joined together to form larger organizations they established their own works for overhauling and building. These company workshops caused places like Crewe (LNWR), Doncaster (GNR), Derby (MR) and Swindon (GWR) to become known as the Railway Towns. Tens of thousands of locomotives were built in these and other towns – over 7,000 in Crewe alone – all for home use rather than export.

The first centre of locomotive building in Britain was established in the mining town of Newcastle in 1821 when George Stephenson and his son Robert opened the world's first workshop dedicated solely to locomotive building. By 1855 the company had built more than 1,000 for Britain and the rest of the world. In 1899 the private company was shut down and a new limited company took its place.

One of the first builders of locomotives in Leeds was Fenton, Murray & Wood. Founded in 1795, their first locomotive, "Prince Regent", was built for Middleton Colliery in 1812. Although the company only built five more

- **ABOVE LEFT**
Charles Beyer (1813–76) of the locomotive building partnership Beyer Peacock.

- **ABOVE RIGHT**
Richard Peacock of the locomotive building partnership Beyer Peacock.

- **LEFT**
Beyer Peacock letterhead.

- **ABOVE**
Works plate from Kitson & Co., Leeds, one of the Leeds builders who made that city famous across the world.

- **ABOVE**
Another great Glasgow builder, Sharp, Stewart, who had moved to Springburn from Great Bridgwater Street in Manchester.

- **ABOVE**
A plate of Falcon Engine and Car Works Company of Loughborough – the forerunner of the famous Brush Works, which continues the tradition of building hi-tech locomotives for today's railway.

● **RIGHT**
A 4-6-0 locomotive built by Robert Stephenson of Newcastle.

● **BELOW LEFT**
The Greek god of Fire used as the symbol for Charles Tayleur & Co., whose works became the famous Vulcan Foundry.

● **BELOW RIGHT**
James Naysmyth, legendary Victorian engineer and founder of Naysmyth Wilson Patricroft Locomotive Works.

locomotives, one of Murray's apprentices, Charles Todd, went on to found his own business, with James Kitson, in 1835. At first they built only parts, but by 1838 they had produced their first complete locomotive. It was so large that they had to pull down one of the workshop walls before it could be delivered.

One of the earliest manufacturers of locomotives in Manchester was William Fairbairn, who had founded an iron foundry in 1816 and who entered into locomotive building in 1839. In 1863, having built about 400 locomotives, the firm was taken over by Sharp, Stewart & Co., a firm which had been established in

● **ABOVE**
Dübs works plate from an early Spanish locomotive.

● **RIGHT**
Henry Dübs, one of the great Glasgow builders, whose works were in Polmadie.

1828 by Thomas Sharp and Richard Roberts. By the 1880s Sharp, Stewart had expanded so much that they left their Manchester foundries and relocated in Glasgow. In 1903 the three firms of Sharp, Stewart, Neilson Reid and Henry Dübs merged to become the North British Locomotive Company Ltd. Another of the great Manchester builders was Beyer, Peacock & Co., which, unlike the companies mentioned so far, had been founded, in 1854, purely as a locomotive building works.

One of the earliest building firms founded in Glasgow was that of Walter Neilson and James Mitchell. Although they had commenced the production of stationary engines in 1830, it was not

until 1843 that they produced their first locomotives. By 1860 the small works could not keep pace with orders, and a new foundry was built in Finniston. Even this factory soon became too small, and in 1861 work began on new premises in Springburn. The firm's locomotives were exported to many countries, including India, South Africa and Argentina. In 1864 Henry Dübs left the company to establish his own locomotive factory at Polmadie. Within three years the firm had achieved such a reputation that it was exporting to India, Cuba, Spain, Finland and Russia.

The great export trade that developed as Britain took railways to many parts of the world continued to be developed by private builders who in turn made cities like Manchester, Leeds, Newcastle and Glasgow famous throughout the world.

EARLY NORTH AMERICAN LOCOMOTIVES

Horse-drawn railways for hauling coal first appeared in the United States of America from about 1826. Then, having heard of events in England, in 1828 a commission of three American engineers visited the works of Robert Stephenson in Newcastle upon Tyne, the great engineering centre, and those of Foster, Rastrick & Co. in Stourbridge, a market-town and manufacturing centre in Worcestershire, west central England. The result of this visit was that, the next year, four locomotives were ordered, one from Stephenson and three from Foster, Rastrick. Stephenson's was delivered first in January 1829, but, for reasons which are unclear, it was not put into service. Foster, Rastrick's Stourbridge Lion arrived next and was the first steam-driven locomotive put into operation in the USA.

● **MATTHIAS BALDWIN**

The second Stephenson locomotive sent to America, a six-wheeler built in 1829, had, like the first, bar-frames. This type of design, soon to be abandoned in

● LEFT
The York was Phineas Davis's winning entry in the 1831 Baltimore & Ohio locomotive competition. Like many early American designs, it featured a vertical boiler – but this style was called a "cheese".

● ABOVE
Ross Winans built vertical-boiler, vertical-cylinder locomotives called "grasshoppers" for the Baltimore & Ohio line, at its Mount Claire Shops, Baltimore, Maryland. In 1927, for its "Fair of the Iron Horse", B&O posed the Andrew Jackson of about 1835 as the Thomas Jefferson.

Britain, remained the standard in America for many years. Stephenson's third, a Planet-type 2-2-0, was delivered to the Mohawk & Hudson Railway (M&HR) in 1832. This was examined by Matthias Baldwin who went on to build Old Ironside, which on its first run reached 30 mph.

At about the same time, Stephenson sent another locomotive to the Camden & Amboy Railroad & Transportation Co. (C&AR&TC). Camden is a seaport in New Jersey, which became a terminus in 1834, Amboy is in Illinois. The locomotive had a circular boiler and domed "haystack" firebox. A year after its arrival, its front wheels were removed and a four-wheeled bogie with a cowcatcher substituted, to make it suitable for local conditions. It entered service in November 1831 at Bordentown, New Jersey. The oldest complete locomotive in the USA, it was brought out of retirement in 1893 to haul a train of two 1836-type C&A passenger-coaches. The train did the 1,481 km (920 miles) from New York City to Chicago in five days.

● LEFT
The De Witt Clinton was built for the Mohawk & Hudson line by the West Point Foundry, New York, in 1831.

● PETER COOPER

In 1830, the Baltimore & Ohio (B&O) line put into service Peter Cooper's Tom Thumb, on the 21 km (13 mile) stretch across Maryland between Baltimore and Ellicott's Mill. This was more of a scientific model than a proper locomotive, but it convinced American business that steam traction was a practical thing. The same year, the West Point Foundry of New York City constructed the first all-American-built locomotive, "The Best Friend of Charleston", for the South Carolina Railroad (SCR). In 1832, the same foundry completed Experiment, later named Brother Jonathan. This, the first locomotive in the USA to incorporate a leading bogie, was also the

first to operate on a regular scheduled run. The locomotive came to a premature end when its vertical bottle-like boiler burst.

In 1831, the De Witt Clinton, built by the West Point Foundry, made her first journey on the M&HR line. The locomotive, with cylinders mounted either side of the footplate's rear, reached 15 mph on the Albany-Schenectady line, which had been built across New York state to connect the two eponymous rivers. It could not have been a successful engine, for it was scrapped in 1835.

● ABOVE AND INSET
Camden & Amboy's first locomotive, John Bull, was built by Stephenson in England. It was assembled in the USA by Isaac Dripps. He added a pilot, making it the first locomotive in America to employ a cowcatcher pilot.

TOM THUMB

Date	1830
Builder	Peter Cooper, New York, USA
Client	Baltimore & Ohio (B&O)
Gauge	4 ft 8½ in
Driving wheels	2-2-0
Capacity	2 cylinders 3 x 14 in

● RIGHT
In 1830, New York businessman Peter Cooper demonstrated the first American-built locomotive on the Baltimore & Ohio railroad. This locomotive was later named Tom Thumb. A 1926 replica poses here.

EARLY BALDWIN LOCOMOTIVES

In 1834, Baldwin, having already built Old Ironside, produced his second engine, the E.L. Miller. This was for the Charleston and Hamburg Railroad (C&HR). Old Ironside's composite wood-and-iron wheels had proved fragile, so Baldwin fitted his six-wheeled machine with solid bell-metal driving wheels of 4 ft 6 in in diameter. A sister locomotive, Lancaster, appeared in June the same year and promptly set an American record by hauling 19 loaded cars over Pennsylvania's highest gradients between Philadelphia and Columbia. This persuaded the railway's directors to adopt steam power instead of horse traction and they placed an order with Baldwin for five more locomotives. The first Baldwin engine to

● LEFT
This Class 152 2-6-0 is typical of early wagontop boilered Moguls from Baldwin. The usual array of fluted and flanged domes, diamond chimney, short smokebox, cross-head-driven boiler-feed pump with back-up injector is completed by a decorated headlight.

have outside-cylinders, the Black Hawk, was delivered to the Philadelphia & Trenton Railroad (P&TR) in 1835.

● POWER DEMANDED
Railways were now demanding more powerful locomotives. Baldwin considered there was no advantage in the

OLD IRONSIDES

Date	1832
Builder	Baldwin, Philadelphia, Pennsylvania, USA
Client	Camden & Amboy Railroad (C&AR)
Gauge	4 ft 8½ in
Driving wheels	4 ft 6 in
Capacity	2 cylinders 9½ x 18 in

● OPPOSITE TOP, INSET
The builder's plate of the Baldwin-built 2-6-0 Mogul No. 20, Tahoe.

● OPPOSITE TOP
Matty Baldwin's first locomotive-building shop, in Lodge Alley, Philadelphia.

● OPPOSITE BOTTOM
The Tahoe, a Baldwin-built 2-6-0 Mogul-type, once operated by the Virginia & Truckee (V&T) line in Nevada, displayed at the Rail-road Museum of Pennsylvania, Stroudsburg, Pennsylvania.

● RIGHT
From the early years, Baldwin built many saddle-tanks of distinctive generic appearance. This veteran, working at the E.G. Lavandero Sugar Mill, Cuba, is typical.

eight-wheeled engine, arguing it would not turn a corner without slipping one or more pairs of wheels sideways. None the less, in May 1837, he built his first eight-wheeler. Baldwin's outside-cylindered 0-8-0 Ironton of 1846 had the two leading coupled axles on a flexible beam truck, allowing lateral motion and the relatively long wheelbase to accommodate itself to curves.

● CONCERNS ABOUT ADHESION
As railroads spread, so 1:50 gradients or steeper were met, bringing concerns about adhesion. Baldwin's initial response was to incorporate a supplementary pair of smaller-diameter wheels on an independent axle, driven by cranks from the main driving wheels. The first such engine was sold to the Sugarloaf Coal Co. in August 1841. On a trial run,

it hauled 590 tons across Pennsylvania from Reading to Philadelphia, a distance of 87 km (54 miles) in 5 hours 22 minutes, yet another American speed-and-haulage record.

Baldwin's classic locomotive development for heavy freightwork was the 2-6-0- Mogul. In this design, he substituted an extra pair of coupled wheels and single carrying-axle for the leading bogie of the classic American 4-4-0 passenger-engine. The result was a machine that could also be turned to passenger work in mountainous country.

Baldwin's earliest locomotives were built at Matty, his modest assembly-shop in Lodge Alley, Philadelphia. The company he formed became the world's largest locomotive-builder. In the 117-year history of Baldwin Locomotives' work more than 7,000 engines were built.

AMERICAN LOCOMOTIVES – 1840–75

The years between 1840 and the American Civil War (1861–5) saw locomotive production treble. By the end of the 1850s, not only were there 11 main American builders but they had also progressed beyond the experimental stage to bulk production of well-defined standard types suited to local conditions.

With the development of the railroad over the Appalachian Mountains, separating the American East from the West, Richard Norris & Son of Philadelphia, Pennsylvania, extended the classic 4-4-0 by adding an extra coupled axle at the rear to become the 4-6-0 type ("Ten-Wheeler"). This allowed a much larger boiler and the extra pair of drivers gave 50 per cent extra adhesion to cope with steep gradients. The use of bar-frames by American locomotive builders allowed the simple enlargement of existing designs without needing to retool or create more workshop capacity.

● **RIGHT**
The Pioneer, a 2-2-2 single-driver "bicycle"-type built in 1851 by Seth Wilmarth for the Cumberland Valley Railroad. This was the first locomotive to operate in Chicago.

● **LEFT**
The railroad depot at Nashville, Tennessee, during the American Civil War.

● **BELOW**
This replica of the Central Pacific Railway's 4-4-0 Jupiter and Union Pacific Railroad's No. 119 stands at the Golden Spike National Monument, Promontory, Promontory Point, Utah.

A typical American express train of the 1860s headed by a 4-4-0. This was the most important type of American locomotive providing the flexibility for running at speeds over lightly laid and often rough track beds.

● MOGULS AND CONSOLIDATIONS

Many American engineers became concerned that the increasing length of locomotive boilers interfered with the driver's view. In 1853 Samuel J. Hayes of the Baltimore & Ohio Railroad (B&OR) built a 4-6-0 with the cab perched on top of the boiler, surrounding the steam dome. It looked strange but the mechanical design was sound. The layout was copied by other builders.

In the 1860s, the New Jersey Railroad Co. (NJRC) was an early customer for the Baldwin 2-6-0 Mogul freight locomotives already described. As line speeds rose and trains became heavier still, an even larger freight engine was needed. In 1866, the Lehigh & Mahoning Railroad (L&MR), eponymous with rivers in Pennsylvania and Ohio, added a leading two-wheeled truck to the 0-8-0 design to create the Consolidation, the name by which heavy-freight 2-8-0s were henceforth known.

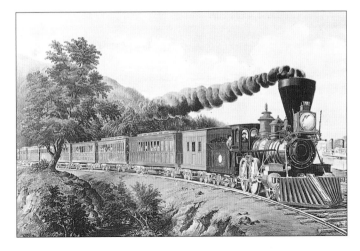

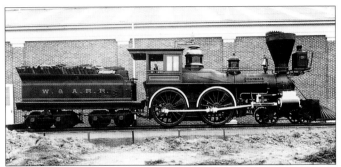

● ABOVE
The 1855 Brooks-built General, owned by the Western & Atlantic Railroad (W&AR), is famous for its role in the American Civil War. It was stolen from the Confederacy by Union spies and involved in a great chase. This is a typical 4-4-0 American-type of the period.

ATLAS

Date	1846
Builder	Baldwin, Philadelphia, Pennsylvania, USA
Client	Philadelphia & Reading
Wheels	0-8-0
Capacity	Cylinders 16½ x 18½ in
Weight	23.7 tons

Transcontinental links were planned in 1862 as part of President Lincoln's aim to unite the North and preserve the Union. As the 1860s ended, the last rails of the Union Pacific Railroad (UPR) and the Central Pacific Railway (CPR) were joined at Promontory, near Ogden, Utah. CPR President Leland Stanford, who had built eastwards from California, drove in the gold spike to fasten the track when the two lines met to form the first American transcontinental railway on 10 May 1869. The event, commemorated by the Golden Spike Monument, linked the Atlantic and Pacific Oceans by rail and left the way open to the large and powerful locomotives that were to come, serving settlement of the West, which now leapt ahead.

AMERICAN LOCOMOTIVES – 1875–1900

Industrialization and modernization meant free time and more spending money for the American workforce to buy things such as day trips and holidays. To meet this demand, in the late 1870s heavy traffic developed, especially weekend travel between Philadelphia and New Jersey. This called for longer passenger-trains and faster schedules.

● AIR-BRAKES AND ANTHRACITE

Until the 1870s, the 4-4-0 engine proved ideal for American railroads. Then, faster, heavier traffic began to demand something larger. Bigger locomotives led to heavier rails, stronger bridges, bigger turntables, better cars, longer passing-loops and, most important of all, air-brakes. George Westinghouse's

● **ABOVE**
The 4-4-0 American type was the universal locomotive from about 1850 to 1895. More than 24,000 were built. On this high-drivered Philadelphia & Reading camelback-design 4-4-0, the engineer rides above the boiler, the fireman behind.

● **LEFT**
The 2-8-0 type was popular with narrow-gauge railroads for high adhesion on mountain rails. This 1881 Baldwin, built for the D&RG, is displayed at the Colorado Railroad Museum, Golden, Colorado.

CHICAGO BURLINGTON & QUINCY 2-4-2	
Date	1895
Builder	Baldwin, Philadelphia, Pennsylvania, USA
Client	Chicago Burlington & Quincy (CB&Q)
Gauge	4 ft 8½ in
Driving wheels	7 ft ¼ in
Capacity	Cylinders 19 x 26 in

● **LEFT**
This 1895 Baldwin-built 36 in gauge 2-8-0 Consolidation-type was typical of locomotives operating in Colorado before the turn of the century. It first operated on the Florence & Cripple Creek Railroad (F&CCR) and later on the Denver & Rio Grande (D&RG). It is displayed at Durango, Colorado.

● LEFT
When built in 1886,
this Baldwin
2-10-0 "Decapod"
was reported to be
the world's largest
locomotive. No. 500
and its sister
No. 501 beat a
temporary track
across the
mountains while a
tunnel was being
completed.

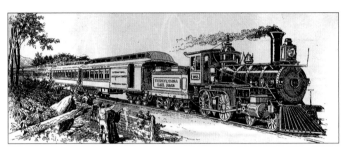

● ABOVE
A 4-4-0 on the Pennsylvania Railroad.

compressed air-brake replaced hand-
brakes almost immediately after he
introduced it in 1868, allowing the high
speed of modern trains.

Baldwin's 5,000th production was
the 4-2-2 Lovett Eames. Built in 1880,
the locomotive was fitted with a wide-
grate Wootten firebox for burning
anthracite coal, a fuel fast replacing coke
and wood. The 6 ft 6 in driving wheels
made the locomotive well suited for
high-speed passenger service: Baldwin
guaranteed it would maintain a 60 mph
average speed pulling four cars. It was
to have been No. 507 of the
Philadelphia & Reading Railroad
(P&RR) but only ran trials before the
railroad went bankrupt and returned it
to her builder.

● "DECAPOD" – WORLD'S LARGEST
LOCOMOTIVE

Six years later, Baldwin produced what
was reported to be the largest locomotive
in the world – a 2-10-0 "Decapod". Its

ten 3 ft 9 in driving wheels were
intended as much for spreading its great
weight over as many axles as possible as
they were for gaining adhesion on a
temporary track over the mountains
while a tunnel was being driven. To
facilitate negotiating tight curves, the
second and third pairs of drivers were
flangeless. A rival claimant for the title of
largest engine in the world was the
4-8-0 Mastodon heavyfreight engine of
the 1890s.

The American type 4-4-0 was eclipsed
on all major railroads by the end of the
century. Its final flowering, in 1893, was
the L Class of New York Central Railroad
(NYCR). That year, No. 999 topped
100 mph at the head of the Empire State
Limited between New York City
and Buffalo.

● BELOW
A 4-4-0 built in 1881 by Sharp, Stewart, of
Glasgow, Scotland, for the St John & Maine
Railroad (SJ&MR), linking St John and Maine.

AMERICAN LOCOMOTIVE BUILDERS

The first British locomotive was imported into the USA in 1829. Within a year the first American-built machine, "The Best Friend of Charleston", from the West Point Foundry of New York City, was on the rails. By the end of the 1830s, about a dozen workshops had tried their hands at locomotive-building. By 1840, as railways were being built or projected in all parts of the USA, the three main American builders – Baldwin, Norris and Rogers – had made 246 locomotives between them, the first two in Philadelphia, the third in New Jersey.

● STANDARDIZATION OF COMPONENTS

In the USA, as in Britain, there were operating-company workshops as well as private builders. Generally, company shops concentrated on repair and main-tenance, leaving building of complete locomotives to private companies. An exception was the Pennsylvania Railroad's Altoona Works, which began locomotive production in 1866 and quickly standardized components within classes. This was a great improvement because, at this time, locomotives were still mainly handbuilt, meaning it was rarely possible to interchange parts, even on locomotives of the same type from the same builder.

● ABOVE
Baldwin's erecting shop (*The American Railway*, 1892).

● BELOW
The William Crooks was the first locomotive to operate in Minnesota. It was built by the New Jersey Machine Works in Paterson, New Jersey, in 1861 for the St Paul & Pacific Railroad (SP&PR), a predecessor of American railway pioneering entrepreneur James J. Hill's Great Northern Railway (GNR). Hill was nicknamed "the Empire Builder".

Rogers Locomotive and Machine Works,

Of PATERSON, N. J.   *New York Office:* **44 EXCHANGE PLACE.**

Manufacturers of

LOCOMOTIVE ENGINES AND TENDERS,

AND OTHER RAILROAD MACHINERY.

J. S. ROGERS, Pres't,
R. S. HUGHES, Sec'y,   } PATERSON, N. J.
WM. S. HUDSON, Sup't,

ROBT. S. HUGHES Treas.

44 Exchange Place New York,

Poor's Manual of Railroads, 1879.

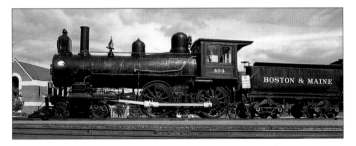

BOSTON & MAINE

● **LEFT**
Rogers Locomotive and Machine Works, of New Jersey, one of the USA's most important. The works produced 6,200 locomotives in the 76 years 1837–1913.

● **ABOVE RIGHT**
A Baldwin builder's plate dated 1878, found on a locomotive shipped to Cuba.

● **BELOW LEFT**
Manchester Locomotives Works, of Manchester, New Hampshire, built this high-drivered 4-4-0 American type for the Boston & Maine Railroad (B&MR).

● **BELOW**
Florence & Cripple Creek Railroad's No. 20, a 36 in gauge Schenectady-built 4-6-0, later used by the Rio Grande Southern Railroad.

● **BOTTOM**
The numberplate for Duluth & Northern Minnesota's No. 14, a Baldwin 2-8-2 Mikado-type built in 1912.

● SPECIALISTS TAILOR-MADE FOR INDUSTRY

Apart from main-line railroads, rail transport was spreading widely across industry, and specialist locomotive-manufacturers sprang up to tailor-make machines for industry's needs. Doyen of these was Ephraim Shay, a sawmill-owner from Haring, Michigan. He brought timber down from forests on temporary, corkscrew tracks. As these could not stand the weight of a conventional locomotive, he designed his own. In 1880, he mounted a boiler in the centre of a flat bogie-car. This was offset to one side, to allow a pair of vertical cylinders to drive a horizontal shaft turning along the locomotive's right-hand side at wheel-centre level. This engine was nothing like a conventional locomotive, but it was perfect for its job.

● VOLUME OUTPUT FROM FACTORIES

Before 1880, most American locomotives were fairly small machines of weights rarely exceeding 30 tons. This meant they could be built in small workshops without the need for big overhead cranes and their bar-frame components could be made by hand in an ordinary black-smith's forge. However, by 1890, loco-motives had grown so much in size that traditional shops had become useless. The largest builders, such as Baldwin and Cook, set up multi-storied factories with heavy-duty power cranes to build locomotives on a volume-production scale. Smaller firms could no longer compete and collapsed financially.

CANADIAN LOCOMOTIVES

Canada's first railway was a wooden tramway in Quebec extending just more than 27 km (17 miles) between Laprairie and St Johns. The line, opened for traffic in 1832, was for combining rail and water transport via the Hudson and Richelieu rivers. In the first winter of operation, the wooden rails were torn up by adverse weather. The next spring, metal rails replaced them.

● AMERICAN ENGINES

In July 1836, the Champlain & St Lawrence Railroad (C&SLR) was opened. Its first train was pulled by horses because the Canadian engineer could not get the English-built locomotive, Stephenson's 0-4-0 Dorchester, nicknamed "Kitten", to work. An engineer from the USA found that all it needed was "plenty of wood and water", and eventually it built up steam and managed an "extraordinary" 20 mph.

Canadian steam locomotives displayed British and American characteristics and the classic American-outline 4-4-0 was popular. Canadian winter conditions could play havoc with the track, and the American design proved more satisfactory than the British-style 2-4-0 with its relatively rigid wheelbase. American 4-4-0s were supplied in quantities to Canada in the 1870s and were regarded as a general-service type.

● ABOVE
The Samson was built in 1838 by Hackworth, of Wylam, Northumberland, in England for use in Canada. It was the first locomotive to operate in Nova Scotia and one of the earliest used in Canada.

● BELOW
The Countess of Dufferin, a typically Canadian 4-4-0, was the first locomotive put into service on the Canadian Pacific Railway (CPR).

A 4-4-0 built in 1870 by Dübs, of Glasgow, Scotland, for the Canadian ICR. Note the ornate headlamp and wheel bosses.

In 1868, a 4-4-0 was built by Neilson of Glasgow, Scotland, for the 5 ft 6½ in-gauge Canadian Grand Trunk Railway (CGTR). The massive spark-arrester chimney top was 6 ft wide.

● COUNTESS OF DUFFERIN

The Countess of Dufferin was built by Baldwin in 1872 and used on governmental contracts in Manitoba, Canada's easternmost Prairie Province, before going to the Canadian Pacific Railway (CPR) in 1883 – the same year the CPR built its first locomotive. Designed by the Scottish engineer F.R.F. Brown, it was a typical "American" type 4-4-0 with 5 ft-2 in coupled wheels. Canada followed American locomotive

practice very closely, but there were subtle differences. The Countess featured a British-style parallel boiler, not the steeply coned American wagon-top pattern; the spark-arresting stack's shape bespoke Canadian rather than American design.

However, the wagon-top boiler did feature in the early Canadian 4-6-0 and 2-8-0 designs. Its provision for additional steam space over the firebox crown, the hottest part of the boiler, helped avoid priming, particularly when locomotives

were tackling the 1:25 gradients of the CPR's Rocky Mountain section. On this section, passenger- and freight-trains were handled by small-wheeled 2-8-0s, loads often limited to no more than two bogie-cars per locomotive. When a long train had to be worked over the mountains, engines were interspersed through the train at two-car intervals. By the end of the 19th century, coal replaced wood as fuel, and the need for hitherto prominent spark-arrester chimneys ceased.

A 4-4-0	
Date	1868
Builder	Neilson, Glasgow, Scotland
Client	Canadian Grand Trunk Railway (CGTR)
Gauge	5 ft 6½ in
Driving wheels	4-4-0
Capacity	Cylinders

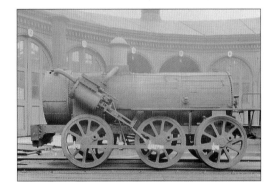

The Albion, often cited as the third locomotive to operate in Canada, was made by Rayne & Burn at Newcastle upon Tyne, England. This locomotive is often misrepresented as a Hackworth product.

EARLY EUROPEAN LOCOMOTIVES

The first locomotive built on mainland Europe was the unsuccessful Berliner Dampfwagen 1, a 0-4-0, constructed in Germany in 1816 for the horse-drawn Köningsgrube Tramway. The first successful steam trials in Europe were on the Saint-Etienne & Lyons Railway in 1828, using a pair of early Stephenson engines. In November 1829, French engineer Marc Séguin put his own engine into service on the line. It had a multi-tubular boiler with huge rotary fans, mounted on the tender and blowing fire through leather pipes. It could pull up to 18 tons but could not exceed 2 mph.

AJAX	
Date	1841
Client	Austrian North Railway
Gauge	1,435 mm
Driving wheels	0-6-0

● **BELOW**
Der Adler, the first steam locomotive used on the Nuremberg-Fürth Railway, Bavaria, on 7 December 1835.

● **ALTERNATING SAWS**
Séguin produced two more locomotives. They went into service but had problems with belt-driven bellows mounted in the tender. These continually broke down from lack of steam. To allow for this, a wagon with four horses always accompanied the locomotive to provide traction should it be needed. These faults were ironed out, and by 1835 Séguin had completed 12 more locomotives of the same type that, because of the action of the levers, were referred to as *scieurs de long*, "alternating saws".

● FIRST IN GERMANY AND THE NETHERLANDS

The inaugural locomotive used in 1835 on Germany's first steam railway, in Bavaria, between Nuremberg and Fürth, was Der Adler. This 2-2-2 Patentee-type, built by Stephenson, had outside-frames and an enormously tall chimney of small diameter. It became popular in Europe and was the first locomotive introduced into several countries, including the Netherlands in 1839 when one opened the country's first line, in North Holland province, between Amsterdam, the commercial capital, and Haarlem 19 km (12 miles) west.

● AUSTRIAN EMPIRE'S FIRST

The first steam railway in the Austrian Empire was the Kaiser Ferdinand Nordbahn, which opened in 1837 using two Stephenson Planet-type locomotives, the Austria and the Moravia. Robert Stephenson's assistant John Haswell (1812–97) accompanied the engines to Vienna and stayed on to take charge of the rail workshops there. He was responsible for much early Austrian locomotive development.

● BRITISH INFLUENCE IN RUSSIA

Russia's first public railway was opened in 1837 between the royal centres of St Petersburg, the capital (1712–1914), and Tsarskoye Selo – "The Tsar's Village" summer residence 24 km (15 miles) south. Its first three locomotives were all Patentee 2-2-2s, one each from Timothy Hackworth, Robert Stephenson & Co. and Tayleur & Co. However, the first Russian-built engine was already at work on an industrial line in the Urals. This was a 2-2-0, built in 1833 by M. Cherepanov, a man who had seen early Stephenson locomotives in action in England.

● **ABOVE**
A Buddicom 2-2-2 locomotive built for the Paris-Rouen Railway in 1843. It could average 38 mph and is pictured arriving for display at the Festival of Britain in London in 1951.

● **BELOW**
Ajax, built by Isambard Kingdom Brunel in 1841 for the Austrian North Railway, entered service on the Floridsdorf-Stockerau stretch of the line, north out of Vienna.

EUROPE – MID-19TH CENTURY

The Alps are a mountain barrier in south Central Europe extending more than 1,000 km (650 miles) from the Mediterranean coast of France and north-west Italy through Switzerland, northern Italy and Austria to Slovenia. Their highest peak is 4,807 m (15,771 ft) Mont Blanc.

From 1844, the Austrian Government built the main line southwards from Vienna over the Alps via the Semmering Pass, 980 m (3,215 ft) above sea level. Engineer Karl Ghega used heavy gradients and severe curvature to conquer this barrier. The 29 km (18 mile) ascent from Gloggnitz to the summit is graded almost continually at 1:40. No existing locomotive was powerful enough to work trains over the pass, and it was at first thought that trains would have to be cable-hauled or worked by atmospheric power. Finally, a German technical magazine suggested a locomotive competition, on the lines of the Rainhill Trials, to find the best design of engine for mountain haulage. The Government Locomotive

● **ABOVE**
Wesel, built in 1851 by Borsig of Berlin, ran on the Cologne-Minden line across what since 1946 has been the Federal German state of North-Rhine Westphalia.

● **BELOW LEFT**
RENFE locomotive No. 030-2016, built by Kitson, Thomson & Hewitson, of Leeds in 1857, is seen here working as a station-pilot at Valencia, eastern Spain, in 1962.

● **BELOW RIGHT**
Gmunden was built in 1854 by Gunther, of the Lower Austrian town of Wiener Neustadt, for the narrow-gauge (1.106 metre) Linz-Gmunden line crossing Upper Austria.

Superintendent, Baron Engerth, agreed. The Semmering Trials were held in July 1851.

● **SEMMERING TRIALS**
Of the four entrants, three became milestone-makers in articulated-locomotive development. All four competitors more than fulfilled the test conditions, climbing the pass with the test-load faster than the required minimum speed. The winner of the first prize of 20,000 gold florins was the German entry Bavaria

Pfalz, a Crampton-type locomotive, was built in 1853 by Maffei of Munich for the Bavarian Palatine Railway. This replica is pictured in front of locomotive sheds at Nuremberg, Bavaria.

LIMMAT

Date	1846
Builder	Emil Kessler, Karlsruhe, Baden, Germany
Client	Swiss Northern
Gauge	1,435 mm
Driving wheels	4-2-0
Capacity	Cylinders 14.25 x 22 mm

locally by Wilhelm Günther.

The railway bought all the engines, and Bavaria was rebuilt in 1852 by Engerth as an 0-6-0 with its tender-frames extended forward to support the firebox's weight. Thus was created the Engerth-type of semi-articulated locomotive, which became popular in Austria, France, Switzerland and Spain. Seraing was progenitor of the double-boiler Fairlie-type articulated. Wiener Neustadt's design led to the Meyer articulated-locomotive layout. Both types achieved worldwide acceptance.

built by Maffei of Munich, a 0-4-4-4 tender-locomotive with rod-coupled groups of driving wheels linked by roller chains. The other entries were Vindobona, a rigid-framed 0-8-0 by John Haswell of Vienna; Seraing, a double-boilered articulated machine by John Cockerill of Belgium; and Wiener Neustadt, a double-bogie articulated with a single boiler, built

● **ANATOLE MALLET**

The first compound engine was built by Swiss-born, French-educated engineer Anatole Mallet (1837–1919) in 1876 for the Bayonne and Biarritz Railway in south-western France. Steam was admitted to a single high-pressure cylinder from where it was exhausted into a larger-diameter low-pressure

cylinder, working twice over. The claimed advantage was fuel efficiency. Right to the end of steam operation, French Railways were strongly committed to compounds. Two-cylinder compounding was developed in Germany by von Borries of Hanover State Railways, who introduced his compound 2-4-0s for express work in 1880.

Limmat, a long-boilered engine built by Emil Kessler of Karlsruhe, Baden, in the German state of Württemberg, was the first locomotive to run from Zurich, Switzerland, to Baden, south-western Germany, on 19 August 1847. The line became known as the "Spanische Brötli Bahn" – a popular type of confectionery.

EUROPE TO 1900

This de Glehn compound running on France's Nord railway is typical of the closing years of the 19th century. Similar engines played a prolific part in express service across France and were also exported to many countries by French and other continental builders.

By 1879, the total track length on Russian railroads was 20,125 km (12,500 miles). Between 1860–90 the ever-growing demand for locomotives could not be met by Russian building alone, and many engines were imported from Britain, France, Germany and Austria. Two features of Russian locomotives of this period were the fully enclosed cabs, giving protection from harsh winters, and the promenade-deck effect, produced by handrails extending round the footplating on either side of the boiler to stop the crew slipping off in icy weather. In 1895, the first of 29 0-6-6-0 Mallet articulated-compound tender-engines was put into service, on the 3 ft 6 in gauge Vologda-Archangel railway in north Russia.

● ALFRED DE GLEHN

Alfred de Glehn (1848–1936), an inspired British engineer working in France as technical chief of Société Alsacienne, evolved a system of compounding using two high- and two low-pressure cylinders. His first

locomotive was an advanced 4-2-2-0 in which the outside high-pressure cylinders were set well back in Crampton fashion and drove the rear-pair of uncoupled wheels. The low-pressure cylinders, set forward between the frames, drove the leading driving-axle. In partnership with Gaston du Bousquet (1839–1910), chief engineer of the Northern Railway of France, bigger, better and faster derivatives with coupled driving wheels were introduced in the 1890s, placing

the Nord at the fore of high-speed locomotive performance. The first four-cylinder de Glehn compound was made in 1886 – the last in 1929.

● KARL GÖLSDORF

Compound locomotives were also developed in Austria by Karl Gölsdorf (1861–1916), engineer to Austrian State Railways – Österreichische Bundes-bahnen (ÖBB). His earliest two-cylinder engines were freight 0-6-0s introduced

● LEFT
One of Europe's early, huge, heavy-hauling 0-8-0 tender-engines from the German builder Hartmann, exported to Spain in 1879.

● ABOVE
This Czech 0-8-0 was originally built in 1893 for the Austrian State Railways as their locomotive No. 73175, by STEG, of Vienna.

EMMETT 2-6-0T	
Date	1886
Builder	Emil Kessler, Karlsruhe, Baden, Germany
Client	Portuguese CN Railway
Gauge	Metre
Driving wheels	3 ft 3½ in
Capacity	Cylinders 13 x 19 mm

in 1893. Gölsdorf's main concern was to provide both passenger- and freight-engines capable of hauling trains over Alpine passes. His heavyfreight 2-8-0s, designed for the Arlberg Tunnel, and of which more than 900 were built, were so successful they lasted in service until the 1950s.

● **CAESAR FRESCOT**

In 1884, Caesar Frescot, chief mechanical engineer (CME) of the Upper Italian Railway, gave Europe its first standard-gauge 4-6-0 tender-locomotive, Vittorio Emanuele II. These locomotives, built at Turin's works, were

● **LEFT**
In 1886 these Emmett light 2-6-0Ts were introduced by builder Emil Kessler, of Karlsruhe, capital of the then state of Baden, for Portugal's metre-gauge lines.

● **BELOW LEFT**
An early Portuguese Railways 5 ft 6 in gauge saddle-tank built by Beyer Peacock, of Manchester, England.

● **BELOW RIGHT**
This type 0-8-0 of the Volga Dam Railway was imported from Britain's Sharp, Stewart in 1871.

intended for heavy passenger and freightwork over the 8 km (5 mile) long Giovi Pass railway tunnel at an altitude of 329 m (1,080 ft), across the Apennine mountain range of central Italy, linking Genoa, Turin and Milan in northern Italy.

They had outside-cylinders and were decorated with much ornamental brasswork, though their appearance was spoilt by the short wheelbase bogie. They were built into the 1890s and lasted well into the 20th century.

EUROPEAN BUILDERS OF THE 19TH CENTURY

One of Europe's first locomotive builders was Matthias von Schönner, the architect of the horse-drawn Budweis & Linz Railway linking the then German-named brewing city of České Budějovice, in southern Bohemia (now Czech Republic) and the Upper Austrian commercial city. Von Schönner visited America in the 1830s and was greatly influenced by the Philadelphian builder William Norris. He returned home to build the Vienna & Raub line which opened in 1842.

The Vienna & Gloggnitz Railway, immediately after opening in 1841,

● ABOVE
European builders, such as Kuntze & Jürdens of Germany, exported their locomotives as far afield as Cuba.

● ABOVE
One of Germany's most prolific locomotive builders was Henschel & Sohn whose works were in Kassel. The company built its first locomotive in 1848. Henschel produced for domestic railways and world export.

● ABOVE
Another prolific world-export market builder was Richard Hartmann, of Chemnitz, a town known as the "Saxon Manchester", standing at the base of the Erzgebirge, the "Ore Mountains" chain.

● ABOVE
The former German builder BMAG of Berlin was initially known as Schwartzkopff, as shown by this ornate maker's plate.

● ABOVE
A lesser-known German builder was Rheinische Metalfabrik of Düsseldorf, capital of North-Rhine Westphalia and commercial hub of the Rhine-Ruhr industrial area. Its name is pictured on a Class 20 2-6-0, built in 1922, of Yugoslav Railway – Jugoslovenske Železnice (JŽ).

● ABOVE
Borsig of Berlin was a prolific builder for home and export markets.

● ABOVE LEFT TO RIGHT
Orenstein & Koppel builder's plates.

● **LEFT**
A 700 mm gauge
0-4-4-0T 4 cylinder
compound Mallet
built by Ducroo
& Brauns of Weesp,
Holland of 1928
on a sugar
plantation in Java.

● **BELOW**
Borsig of Berlin were a prolific builder for
both the home and export market. One of
their products is this, the world's last surviving
steam tram.

● **BELOW**
Arthur Koppel set up his foundry to produce
large railway equipment in 1885, leading to
creation of Orenstein & Koppel, Germany's
principal builder of narrow-gauge industrial
locomotives. This is an original Arthur Koppel
engine of 1898. She is the 0-4-0 well-tank Laurita
and bears a plate stating "Primera Locomatora
Chacao Paraguayo", that is "first locomotive on
the Paraguayan Chaco" – the Gran Chaco being
the south-central South American plain of huge
swamps and scrub forest covering 780,000 sq
km (300,000 sq miles).

erected its own works to maintain its existing engines and to build new ones. The Scottish engineer John Haswell was in charge and his first locomotive, Wien, was built the same year. In 1842 Wenzel Günther, who worked with Haswell, left to take over as manager of the Wiener Neustadt locomotive works. In 1844, Haswell produced the first 4-4-0 for the Vienna & Gloggnitz. This was followed by his two famous locomotives Grosse Gloggnitzer and Kleine Gloggnitzer. Such was the former's success that it hauled 160 ton passenger-trains and 380 ton freight-trains between Mürzzuschlag, south-west Wiener Neustadt, and Leibach.

● **AUGUST BORSIG**

August Borsig's first locomotive, built in Berline-Moabit, was completed in July 1841 for use on the Berlin & Anhalt Railway, linking the then Prussian capital with the then duchy Prussia surrounded by Saxony. In this production he sought to improve on the American Norris 4-2-0 design by adding a pair of trailing-wheels behind the firebox. This helped weight distribution but robbed the engine of vital adhesive weight on the driving-axle. In his 2-2-2 locomotive Beuth of 1843, also for the Berlin & Anhalt, Borsig embodied the best of English locomotive practice of the time, owing much to Edward Bury but with Stephenson's inclined outside-cylinders.

Borsig went on to become one of Germany's most prolific locomotive factories, supplying a worldwide market.

The firm of Henschel & Sohn, founded in 1817 and based in Kassel, then the capital of Westphalia before becoming part of the Prussian province of Hesse-Nassau, built its first locomotive, Drache (Dragon), in 1848. It was a 4-4-0 of hybrid appearance, combining the Stephenson long-boiler and haystack-firebox with the short-wheelbase Norris leading-bogie. Henschel's output was quite modest – no more than eight engines a year up to 1860 when its 50th locomotive emerged. After the works was extended in 1865, production soared.

INDIAN LOCOMOTIVES

India's first stretch of railway was part of the Great Indian Peninsular Railway (GIPR) between Bombay City and Thana, Maharashtra, 34 km (21 miles) away. It opened in April 1853. For the opening, Tayleur's Vulcan factory at Newton-le-Willows supplied eight inside-cylindered 2-4-0s with domeless boilers, haystack-fireboxes and 5 ft driving wheels.

Just as the GIPR originated in Bombay, so the East Indian Railway (EIR) began in Calcutta. In 1862, ten 2-2-2 express-locomotives with outside-cylinders were built for EIR priority train services. Large canopies over the cabs protected crews from the sun's heat and glare. Their 6 ft 6 in driving wheels equipped them for high-speed running, and they had surprisingly large tenders. The firebox was also relatively large for the period, having an 18 sq ft grate area.

● LEFT
The Indian metre-gauge Class E was an 0-4-2 mixed-traffic version of the D Class. Between 1874–91, 147 examples of a standard design entered service.

● **WESTERN GHATS OBSTACLE**

From its start, the GIPR had problems operating trains over the 900-1,500 m (3,000-5,000 ft) high Western Ghat range. Banking over the mountains' zigzag inclines with heavy tank-engines was common practice. In 1862, Sharp, Stewart & Co., of Glasgow, Scotland, built a tough-looking outside-framed 4-6-0 saddle-tank to the requirements of GIPR engineer J. Kershaw. The first engine of this wheel arrangement to be built in a British works, it was fitted with

sledge-brakes. These were applied to the rails during descent of the western escarpments of the hills where gradients reached 1:37. It was superseded in 1891 by a massive 59 ton 0-8-0ST from the Vulcan Foundry and Neilson of Glasgow.

Webb's three-cylinder compounds were much admired in some quarters, despite precocious behaviour on Britain's LNWR. It may have been that, seen from India, distance lent enchantment to their engineering peculiarities. So it was that the Oudh & Rohilkhand Railway (ORR),

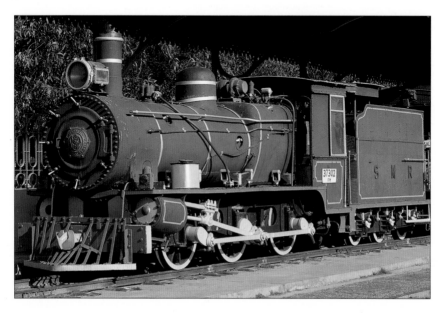

● LEFT
The metre-gauge F Class 0-6-0 dominated Indian railways and is one of the most celebrated locomotive types in world history. The engines worked on many railways. More than 1,000 examples were constructed with little more than detailed variations, between 1884–1922 by 12 different builders.

The Indian metre-gauge Class D 0-4-0 was a standard design comprising ten engines built at Sharp, Stewart's Great Bridgewater Street Foundry, Manchester, England, in 1873.

in what today is the state of Uttar Pradesh, ordered a 5 ft 6 in gauge version from Dübs of Glasgow in 1883. Despite different cab and valve arrangements, it closely resembled the Crewe original, right down to the uncoupled driving wheels.

● **BENGAL-NAGPUR LEADS DEVELOPMENT**

In the late 19th century, Indian broad-gauge locomotive practice often mirrored that on British main lines with 4-4-0s for passenger work and 0-6-0s for goods. Increasing train weights, however, pressed for the development of the small-wheeled six-coupled engine into something rather bigger for Indian conditions. Hence, the Bengal-Nagpur Railway, which linked Calcutta and the capital of the Central Provinces (later Madhya Pradesh) and was always at the fore of technical development, commissioned a class of mixed-traffic 4-6-0s, delivered between 1888–91. Aside from their headlamps and cowcatchers, they were of typical British appearance with straight running-plates, outside-cylinders and inside valve-gear.

● LEFT
The coat of arms of India's Bengal-Nagpur Railway (BNR).

● LEFT
The most celebrated of all Indian 2 ft gauge designs are the 0-4-0 saddle-tanks built for the Darjeeling Railway from 1889. The line took Bengal government officials to their hot-weather headquarters.

● BELOW
The metre-gauge O Class 4-4-0 was an outside-cylinder version of the early M Class. It was the standard passenger-engine on most lines. Some were superheated. The class totalled 297 examples, from six different builders between 1883–1912.

F CLASS 0-6-0

Date	1874
Builder	Various: Britain, Germany, India
Client	Various: Indian State Railways
Gauge	Metre
Driving wheels	3 ft 6 in
Capacity	Cylinders 13 x 20 in
Weight in full working order	20 tons

CHINESE LOCOMOTIVES

China's first railway was opened in 1876 in the eastern province of Kiangsu. It was an 8 km (5 mile) long stretch of 2 ft 6 in gauge between Shanghai and Wusung, Shanghai's outport, that is a subsidiary port built in deeper water than the original port. The first locomotive on the line was the Pioneer, built by Ransomes & Rapier of Ipswich, Suffolk, England. Used by the railway's builders, this 1½ ton engine with 1 ft 6 in driving wheels had a service-truck attached on which the driver sat. The line had a short history. After it had operated for only a month, a local man was fatally injured. Riots ensued and the line was closed. A few months later, it was reopened with two 9 ton 0-4-2STs, Celestial Empire and Flowery Land, both with outside-cylinders and 2 ft 3 in wheels. On these locomotives the water-tanks, a combination of side and saddle, completely enveloped the boiler but left the smokebox clear. However, by the end

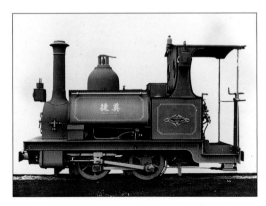

ROCKET OF CHINA

Date	1881
Builder	C.W. Kinder
Client	Kaiping Tramway
Gauge	Narrow gauge
Driving wheels	0-6-0
Capacity	Cylinders 14.25 x 22 mm

of 1877, the Chinese authorities ordered line and engines dismantled.

● KAIPING TRAMWAY

The next attempt to provide a railway in China was in 1881 in the northern province of Hopeh. A mining company built the narrow-gauge Kaiping Tramway as an 8 km (5 mile) link between the Kaiping coalfield near Tangshan, north of Tientsin, and the canal that connected with the Pehtang River. At first, because of Chinese prejudices against steam locomotion, mule traction was used. C.W. Kinder, the company's resident engineer, decided nonetheless to build a steam locomotive. Using odds and ends recovered from various scrap-heaps, he secretly built a small 2-4-0 locomotive, which he named Rocket of China. When the Chinese authorities heard about the locomotive, they sent a commission to investigate. Forewarned of their imminent arrival, Kinder dug a pit and buried his engine.

● THE CHINESE IMPERIAL RAILWAY

In 1886 Dübs & Co. of Glasgow, Scotland, built two 0-4-0STs for a 2 ft gauge section of the Imperial Chinese Railway (ICR). Named Speedy Peace and Flying Victory, they were instantly opposed by the Chinese, who were convinced that the

● ABOVE
The Kaiping Tramway in Hopeh Province was China's first permanent railway. The 2-4-0 Rocket of China pictured here was built in China by British engineer C.W. Kinder and was the tramway's first locomotive.

● RIGHT
Sung Wu Railway
2-4-2T No. 2 was
built by Brooks
Locomotive Works,
Dunkirk, New York,
USA. This celebrated
American builder
produced more than
4,000 locomotives
until it combined
with seven others in
1901 to form the
American
Locomotive
Company (Alco).

● RIGHT
A 2-6-2 saddle-tank built by Dübs in 1887
entered service on the Tientsin Railway in
Hopeh Province.

"devil's machines" would desecrate
ancestral graves. To prevent this, many
trains were halted by Chinese being
thrown in front of the locomotives. Many
were run over and killed. After about 20
of these deaths, the line was eventually
closed and the locomotives scrapped.

● BELOW
This engine is an example of how American
locomotives exported to China exerted
permanent influence on developments. It was
built by Baldwin in 1899 and was No. 230 on
the Chinese Eastern Railway (CER). Although
the CER was operated by Russians, most of its
motive power was of American origin. No. 230
was one of 121 Vauclain compound 2-8-0s
built for the line by Baldwin in 1899. Samuel
Vauclain (1856–1940) worked for Baldwin for
51 years, becoming chairman in 1929. He
invented his compounding system in 1899.

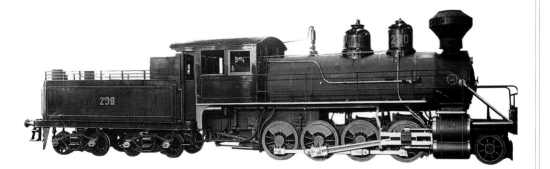

EAST ASIAN RAILWAYS

In Malaya, the first train service started in 1885 in Perak State, between Taiping and Port Weld. Then, in 1886, the first section of the metre-gauge Perak Government Railway (PGR), the 11 km (7 mile) stretch between Kelung and Kuala Lumpur, Perak's capital, was opened. The railway came when the country was covered in dense jungle and transport was entirely by river. The first locomotive was a little 0-6-0 tank by Ransomes & Rapier, of Ipswich, Suffolk, England, similar to the Pioneer and one of the few built by the firm. Small tank-engines were the most suitable for the infant railway system, with the Class A 4-4-0Ts favoured. The larger B Class engines of 1890 were later developed into a tender-engine version. Malayan locomotives were distinguished by their huge headlight – a necessary item on line in dark jungle. Nonetheless, one of these locomotives was charged and derailed by a bull elephant, which lifted the tender clear off the track.

● SINGAPORE-PENANG

By 1909 passengers could travel by train between Singapore and Penang. Completion of the Johore Causeway in

1923 brought the line into Singapore. Singapore had had a railway from Tank Road to Bukit Timah since 1903. In eastern Malaya, goods and passengers could go by train from Gemas to Kota Bharu from 1931.

● BRITISH INFLUENCE IN JAPAN

Japan's first line was built by British engineers in 1872. The first locomotive, a 14¼ ton 2-4-0T with 4 ft 3 in driving wheels, to run on the 3 ft 6 in gauge line was built in 1871 by the Vulcan Foundry of Newton-le-Willows, England. The early equipment on Japanese railways was almost entirely British and included some outside-cylinder 4-4-0s supplied by Dübs & Co. of Glasgow. Other British locomotives to run in Japan were made

● **RIGHT**
A 3 ft 6 in-gauge 4-4-0 engine with inside-cylinders, built in 1899 for the Imperial Government Railways of Japan, by Neilson, of Glasgow, Scotland.

● **OPPOSITE CENTRE**
Another Indonesian State railwy B5014, also from Sharp, Stewart's foundry in 1884, wheezes along the Madian Slahung line. Burning both coal and wood the engine issues shrouds of fire from its chimney.

by Sharp, Stewart of Manchester and by Kitson of Leeds.

One of Kitson's creations was a 0-6-0 goods-engine built in 1873, which three years later was rebuilt in the shops at Kobe, Honshu, as a 4-4-0, a type which became the standard Japanese passenger-locomotive. In 1876 Kitson built another 4-4-0, of typical British appearance, its only oriental feature being the small louvred shutter in the cab side. Class 1800s were introduced in 1881. These engines were fitted with smart copper-capped chimneys bearing the number in brass.

● **AMERICAN INFLUENCE IN JAPAN**
In 1897, Baldwin exported to Japan the Mikado-type. These were the first locomotives built with a 2-8-2 wheel arrangement with a tender. Named in honour of the Japanese head of state, these locomotives were designed to burn an inferior quality of coal,

requiring a large grate area and a deep, large firebox.

One of Japan's steepest railways, up to 1:40 gradient, was the Hakone line serving the eponymous mountain resort near Mount Fuji, on Honshu. For this, Moguls were bought from Rogers in 1897. Japanese railways were Americanized even more in 1900 by the introduction of Schenectady-built 4-4-0s.

● **JAVA**
Perhaps East Asia's most remarkable railway system was on Java whose network serving the islands was developed during the Dutch East Indies

period. The main lines were developed in the last 20 years of the 19th century. Innumerable feeder lines, known as steam tramways, joined them. A gauges battle occurred between the 3 ft 6 in gauge and the standard. For a while, a third rail was laid over the 4 ft 8½ in gauge to enable through 3 ft 6 in gauge trains to operate. The gauge was finally standardized at 3 ft 6 in.

The multiplicity of state and private enterprises that built Java's railways produced a wide diversity of motive power primarily of Dutch, German and British origin.

● **LEFT**
A rare example of Java's standard-gauge network of the NISM, that is Nederlandse Indische Spoorwegen Maatschappij. These 0-6-0 goods-engines, from Beyer Peacock, of England, resemble that company's Ilfracombe goods class. This rare veteran was pictured at Indonesia's southern Javan city of Yogyakarta.

● **BELOW**
The standard O Class outside-cylinder 4-4-0 of the metre-gauge lines of the Indian subconti-nent heading the Royal Train on the Burma State Railway.

INDONESIAN STATE RAILWAYS (ISR) B50 CLASS 2-4-0	
Date	1880
Builder	Sharp, Stewart, Manchester, England
Client	Staats Spoorwegen
Gauge	3 ft 6 in
Driving wheels	1,413 mm
Capacity	Cylinders 381 x 457 mm

AUSTRALASIAN RAILWAYS

In the 19th century, Australia consisted of a series of separate colonies, all with administrations operating independently of each other. This, added to personalities and poor communications, led to the mess of gauge problems from which the country has suffered ever since.

The first steam locomotive to run in Australia was locally built by Robertson, Martin, Smith & Co. It entered service on the Colony of Victoria's Melbourne and Hobsons Bay Railway on 12 September 1854. New South Wales (NSW) followed by opening a 21 km (13½ mile) line from Sydney to Parramatta on 26 September 1855.

● **DIFFICULT TERRAIN**
Australian locomotive design was much governed by the difficult country to be traversed with mountainous country close to coast. The standard gauge in NSW had many 1:30 gradients with curves as tight as 8-chains radius on the main lines. Branch and narrow-gauge states' lines were even worse.

Early locomotives that became standards were generally of the 4-4-0 or 0-6-0 wheel arrangements and of British design or styling. Australia's most significant development was probably the

● **BELOW**
Baldwin supplied ten K(294) Class goods engines in 1885. They were put on lesser duties, including working water-trains between Lake Menindee and Broken Hill mining-town in NSW's dry west. The large wagon behind the locomotive is a 32,000 litre (7,000 gallon) water "gin" to augment the tender's supply.

● **ABOVE**
One of South Australia's Y Class "Colonial Moguls" introduced in 1886. This class originally totalled 134 examples, 58 of which were converted to YX Class with higher-pressure boilers from 1907.

CLASS K TANK	
Date	1892
Builder	Neilson Reid
Client	Western Australian Government Railways (WAGR)
Gauge	3 ft 6 in
Driving wheels	2-8-4
Capacity	Cylinders 19 x 24 in

● OPPOSITE TOP
"Number 10" was the first locomotive built in NSW. She was a 2-4-0 designed on the Stephenson long-boiler principle. Completed in 1870, she was used as an express passenger-locomotive. She is pictured at Picton Station, south-west of Sydney, soon after entering service.

4-6-0 type, well before Jones introduced it to the Highland Railway in Britain. The 30 R Class was introduced from 1886 in South Australia. The P6 Class introduced in NSW in 1892 eventually numbered 191 units.

On the narrow gauge, Beyer, Peacock's development of the "Colonial Mogul" had the most impact, with 134 Y Class in South Australia, 47 G Class in Western Australia and 28 C Class in Tasmania.

● NEW ZEALAND'S GAUGES
New Zealand also started with a mess of gauges. South Island had a 3 ft gauge horse-drawn railway from Nelson, in 1862; a 5 ft 3in gauge steam railway from Christchurch in 1863; a wooden-railed line, worked unsuccessfully on the Davies

or Prosser principle, from Invercargill in 1864; and a 4 ft 8½ in gauge steam-line from Invercargill in 1866. Finally, the 3 ft 6 in gauge was selected as standard and introduced, with double Fairlie loco-motives, at Dunedin in September 1872.

New Zealand had, as well as regular designs, a great variety of types: vertical-boilered locomotives, single- and double-Fairlies, flangeless Prosser-types, Fell locomotives and locally made curiosities. Mainly, short lines radiated from coastal ports, so the most significant design would have been the 88-strong F Class 0-6-0T saddle-tanks.

American locomotives were more successful in New Zealand, starting with eight K Class supplied by Rogers Locomotive works in 1878.

● ABOVE
A New Zealand Government Railways (NZGR) 1873-built A Class 0-4-0 tank by Dübs. These little engines, nicknamed "Dodos", worked well and lasted into the 1920s.

● RIGHT
One of 77 members of the New South Wales (NSW) A(93) Class 0-6-0s, shunting at Sydney's Darling Harbour goods yard.

SOUTHERN AFRICAN RAILWAYS

South Africa's first public railway was a 3 km (2 mile) stretch in Natal between Durban and The Point, opened in June 1860. The locomotive was the "Natal". It was built by Carrett Marshall & Co., of Leeds, England, stripped down, crated and sent to Durban, where it was rebuilt by Henry Jacobs. The engine had a large dome cover and its chimney, of typical American design, incorporated a wire-mesh spark-arrester. This locomotive,

● LEFT
South Africa's first steam locomotive, which operated in Cape Province, was a contractor's engine for building the Cape Town – Wellington Railway in 1859. She was built by Hawthorn & Co.'s works in Leith, Scotland, as a 4 ft 8 in gauge 0-4-2. Here is the preserved veteran, proclaimed a national monu-ment in 1936.

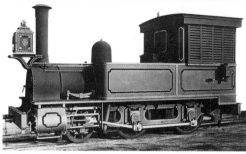

● LEFT
The first locomotive to serve the Ugandan Railway was this Dübs 2-4-0T, one of two locomotives bought secondhand from Indian State Railway (ISR). Dübs of Glasgow built 25 of these engines in 1871–2.

CLASS 6	
Date	1893
Builder	Dübs, of Glasgow, Scotland
Client	Cape Government Railway (CGR)
Gauge	3 ft 6 in
Driving wheels	4 ft 6 in
Capacity	Cylinders 17 x 26 in
Weight in full working order	80 tons

however, was not the first to run in South Africa, for in September 1859, E. & J. Pickering had imported a 0-4-2 built by Hawthorn & Co. of Leith, Scotland.

● **KITSON VERSUS FAIRLIE**
In 1875, the Cape Government Railway (CGR) introduced a back-to-back from Kitson & Co. of Leeds, Yorkshire, and a

0-6-0+0-6-0 Fairlie-type from Avonside Engine Co. of Bristol. In 1864, Robert Fairlie introduced his double-ender. This could be driven in either direction and was adopted in hilly countries where curves and gradients challenged ordinary locomotives. When the two machines were tested against each other, the Fairlie worked around curves with facility, up

● **RIGHT**
The Class 6s were one of the most important types in South African locomotive history. Between 1893–1904, almost all the 268 engines being built to a basic design came from Glasgow. They operated express passenger-trains across the entire republic, with the exception of Natal.

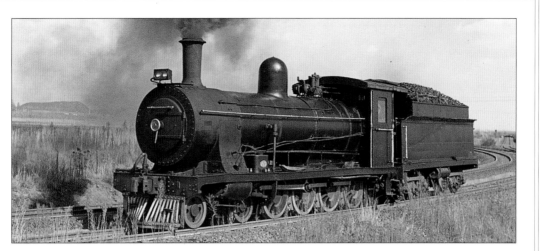

and down gradients, and the Kitson lurched badly descending a decline and was much heavier on fuel.

In 1887, Black Hawthorn, of Gateshead, County Durham, England, built a woodburning 0-4-2ST for the Cape of Good Hope & Port Elizabeth 3 ft 6 in gauge line. It had spark-arrester rails above the tank for wood storage, single slide-bars and Ramsbottom safety-valves with single exhaust.

● EAST AFRICAN LINES

The two pioneer public railways in East Africa were Kenya's Mombasa & Nairobi laid in 1896 and the Usambara Railway through the eponymous highlands of

Tanga Province of German East Africa (later Tanganyika) on which work began in 1893 but was not completed until 1911. A private railway was built from Tanga to Sigi, to serve the logging interests of the Deutsche Holtzegesellschaft für Ostafrika. The first engine used on this line, naturally a woodburner, was a 0-4-2 tank built in 1893 by Vulcan of Stettin, then capital of Pomerania, a province of Prussia.

In May 1896 the first locomotives were delivered to the Ugandan Railway. They were secondhand 2-4-0Ts, bought from Indian State Railways (ISR), built in 1871 by Dübs of Glasgow, Scotland.

● **ABOVE**
The Cape Government Railway (CGR) Class 7 was a small-wheeled freight version of the Class 6 passenger-locomotive. It was introduced in 1892. More than 100 were built, all by the three Glasgow builders Dübs, Neilson and Sharp, Stewart.

● **BELOW**
These locomotives began as main-line 4-10-2Ts on the Natal Government Railway (NGR). They were among more than 100 engines built by Dübs in Polemadie, Glasgow. Replaced by tender-engines, they were converted to 4-8-2Ts for further use as shunting- and trip-engines.

NORTHERN AFRICAN RAILWAYS

Although the first steam tramway in North Africa was built at Egypt's El Dikheila quarries near Alexandria as early as 1838, the first public railway in the region was the British-built Cairo-Alexandria line opened in 1854. By 1870, Egyptian State Railway (ESR) took delivery of a mixed collection of 241 locomotives of over 50 classes supplied by 16 builders from five countries. Besides the usual types, there were a few exotic 2-2-4T saloon locomotives to carry visiting royalty.

● F.H. TREVITHICK'S IN THE NILE VALLEY

British occupation of the Nile Valley in 1882 put railways under the direction of F. H. Trevithick, grandson of the Cornish pioneer. The first new locomotives he introduced were Great Western in concept, with inside-cylinders and strong double-frames. These frames were essential to negotiate Egypt's rough tracks. For the lightest and fastest duties, he ordered 25 2-2-2s from Kitson and the Franco-Belge Company of La Coyère. These sturdy locomotives were the last singles to work in Africa. Some were still in use in World War II.

MOGUL	2 - 6 - 0
Date	1891
Builder	Baldwin, Philadelphia, Pennsylvania, USA
Client	Bône-Guelma Railway, Algeria
Gauge	3 ft 6 in
Driving wheels	4 ft
Capacity	Cylinders 18 x 22 in

● **ABOVE**
A type 0-6-0 tender built by North British, of Glasgow, Scotland, for ESR. The driving wheels are 5 ft ¼ in diameter, the cylinders of 18 x 24 in capacity.

● BELOW
Built by Neilson, of Glasgow, Scotland, this design was on display at the Great Exhibition of 1862, where it was seen by Said Pasha, Viceroy of Egypt, who later ordered one for Egyptian State Railways (ESR).

● FRENCH DESIGN FOR ALGERIA

Algeria's railway development was put in the hands of the French Paris, Lyons & Mediterranean Company in 1863. Secondhand PLM 0-6-0s of characteristic French design were shipped to get services started. Some of these redoubtable 0-6-0 designs, as SNCFA classes 3B, 3E and 3F, were destined to last almost until the end of steam on the Algerian standard gauge. The Algiers-Oran main line opened in 1871 when more 0-6-0s were supplied, with the first of the successful 0-8-0 goods-engines of classes 4A and 4C for the 1:80 gradients up from Philippeville. Operations between Algeria and Tunisia were begun with 0-6-0s built by Batignolles. By 1883, 39 of these, assisted by 18 0-6-0Ts built by the same firm for shunting and banking, were in operation. On the 300 km (184 mile) of the Algerian Western, the sparse service was operated by 26 0-6-0s that were built by Fives Lille and SACM. These ultimately became SNCFA classes 3L and 3M. In 1899 the Bône-Guelma Railway in eastern Algeria turned to Baldwin for ten of its ready-made American-style Moguls. These performed well but were rebuilt as tank-engines in the early 20th century.

● BRITISH PRESENCE IN TUNISIA

Tunisia's first railway was built with British capital and equipment, as part of a move to extend British influence in the region. The standard-gauge line was opened from Tunis to La Marsa in 1874 using four little Sharp, Stewart 2-4-0 tanks. The Italians took over the line in 1876 and ran it until it was acquired by Algeria's Bône-Guelma Co. in 1898. In 1895, under Bône-Guelma's auspices, an extensive metre-gauge network was inaugurated along the coastal region south of Tunis. As motive power, a fleet of no fewer than 135 Mallet articulated engines was built – the largest concentration of these tank-engines in Africa. The first batch of eight 0-4-4-0s came from Batignolles to start services, and larger machines were delivered early in the new century.

SOUTH AMERICAN RAILWAYS

• LEFT
The 4-4-0 was the classic locomotive type in the first few decades of railroading in America, because it provided a good turn of speed and stability over inevitably roughly laid tracks. This example, from the 1840s-50s, was exported to Chile and is pictured in Santiago.

In 1836, three Baldwin locomotives were exported to Cuba, then a Spanish territory. These would have been for the line between the capital, Havana and the small town of Bejueal in La Habana Province. It opened in July 1837.

• ARGENTINE CAUTION

Railways came to Argentina in 1857 when a line opened between the towns of Parque and Floresta. The line manager had so little faith in his own product that he rode on horseback to the opening rather than trust himself to his own railway. The four-wheeled engine used on this occasion was La Portena, a locomotive which had been used in the Crimea, Ukraine.

• AMERICAN INFLUENCE IN BRAZIL

The first railway in Brazil, a short 5 ft 3 in gauge line in the neighbourhood of Rio de Janeiro, the then capital, opened in 1854. The inaugural train was hauled by the 2-2-2 Baroneza. The bulk of Brazil's railway track was laid to metre gauge, though in 1889 the Huain railway was built to the peculiar gauge of 3 ft 1¼ in. Most Brazilian woodburning locomotives of the 19th century were supplied by American builders. Typical was a series of relatively small 2-8-0s from Baldwin with driving wheels of only 3 ft 1 in diameter.

B CLASS	
Date	1906
Builder	Beyer, Peacock, Manchester, England
Client	Buenos Aires and Great Southern (BAGS)
Gauge	5 ft 6 in
Driving wheels	6 ft
Capacity	Cylinders 19 x 26 in (high pressure) 27½ x 26 in (low pressure)
Weight in full working order	115 tons

• BELOW
This classic 4-6-0 two-cylinder compound was built by Beyer, Peacock for the British-owned 5 ft 6 in gauge Buenos Aires and Great Southern Railway (BAGS). These locomotives were a principal express-passenger type for many years.

• LEFT
Another early 4-4-0, almost certainly of European origin and sporting a cowl, is pictured heading a tourist-train in the desert border region between Tacna in Peru and Arica in Chile, disputed territory until 1930.

● MEXICAN CHOICES

In Mexico, a 424 km (265 mile) line opened in 1873 between the capital Mexico City and the seaport Veracruz. The railway was an early user of double-boilered Fairlie 0-6-6-0 tanks. These were successful, unlike the totally impractical American-built Johnstone articulateds of 1888. These were so large they had to be partly dismantled to pass through the 2,608 m (8,560 ft) high Raton Tunnel, Colorado, during delivery. The Mexicans, ever willing to try another form of flexible wheelbase engine, in 1890 bought two Baldwin Mason-Fairlie articulated 2-6-6 tanks. This engine was essentially an American interpretation of the single Fairlie principle, with a power-bogie and a trailing-truck supporting a large boiler with deep firebox.

● ABOVE
Numberplate and worksplate of the Leopoldina Railway.

● RIGHT
This metre-gauge 2-6-0 was one of a class of 15 engines built by Beyer, Peacock of Manchester, England, at the end of the 19th century for Brazil's Leopoldina Railway. The Leopoldina system, all on the metre gauge, has approximately 3,200 km (2,000 miles) of track and was owned by the British-controlled Leopoldina Railway Co.

The Golden Age 1900–50

The first half of the 20th century may truly be called the Golden Age of railways. The railway was the primary form of transport for moving people and freight. The railway was perceived as being the heartbeat of society. Furthermore, throughout the period the vast majority of the world's railways were powered by steam. The period began with a legacy of modest 19th century locomotive designs, which rapidly gave way to 20th century concepts – larger, heavier and more powerful engines, which by the advent of World War II had evolved almost to the ultimate potential within the existing loading gauges. One of the many precepts that accelerated the world change from steam to modern forms of traction was that the necessary power and speeds demanded by railway administrations were outstripping the capacity of steam within the physical restrictions imposed on it.

● **OPPOSITE**
One of Germany's magnificent unrebuilt Reichbahn Standard 01-class Pacifics seen in the soft countryside north of Dresden, Saxony, with an express from Berlin. The Pacific is pictured in charge of a 450-ton train. Coal-fired, these engines operated on timings faster than a mile a minute and were Europe's last high-speed steam expresses.

● **ABOVE**
In the late 19th century the principle of compounding was adopted by many railways throughout the world. Shortly after the turn of the century, Britain's Midland Railway produced a set of 4-4-0s in which two high-pressure cylinders exhausted into a larger low-pressure one. Building continued after the grouping under the London, Midland & Scottish (LMS) Railway and the Midland. Compounds have gone down in locomotive history as one of the most successful classes and remained in Britain until their demise in the 1950s.

BRITISH MAIN-LINE LOCOMOTIVES – PASSENGER

● **BELOW**
The 4-6-0 manifested in both inside- and outside-cylinder form. The former type shown here is one of Holden's Great Eastern engines introduced in 1911 with 6 ft 6 in-diameter wheels, which gave them speed over the flat lands of eastern England.

The turn of the century saw the elegance of the Atlantic-type locomotive established on the main lines of Britain. The type soon led to the Pacific, which in essence was an Atlantic with an extra pair of driving wheels. When Gresley introduced his A1 Pacifics to the Great Northern Railways (GNR) in 1922, they represented in terms of size and power as large an increase over the GN's biggest Atlantic as the first Atlantics of 1898 exerted over the earlier 4-4-2 singles. The Pacific represented the end of the evolutionary line. Nothing bigger ever appeared in Britain, apart from Gresley's incursions into huge 2-8-2 Mikados and his solitary 4-6-4.

The Pacific captured the popular imagination, especially during the competition for Scottish traffic over

Britain's East and West Coast routes in the early 1930s. Worldwide, the streamlined Pacifics of this decade generated much publicity. Gresley's A4s proved to be the "Concordes" of their day and have become the most celebrated British locomotive type. No. 4468

Mallard achieved the world speed record for steam traction of 126 mph in 1938.

The Pacific as an express passenger locomotive was backed up by the 4-6-0, which began to become profuse after the turn of the century. By 1923, the 4-6-0 in both two- and four-cylinder form was

● **RIGHT**
In the 1920s, need arose for an extra passenger locomotive on Britain's Southern Railway, one able to work a 500-ton train at an average speed of almost one mile a minute. So, four-cylinder Lord Nelsons were introduced. They totalled a class of 16 engines named after famous British Sea Lords. These engines worked the Continental Expresses between Victoria Station, London, and the English channel port of Dover, and served the south-western sections of Britain's Southern network.

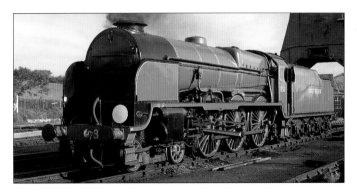

widespread, largely replacing the Atlantic. Not until 1933 did the first Stanier Pacific take the title of the most powerful express-passenger-locomotive type away from the 4-6-0. In 1930, the 4-4-0 made its last flourish with Britain's Southern Railway's three-cylinder Schools engine, the most powerful of this wheel arrangement ever to run in the country.

From the mid-1930s, the 4-6-0 became increasingly used as the basis for

powerful mixed-traffic types. In this guise, it continued to play an important role in main-line passenger duties. With Britain's policy of frequent and relatively light trains, the 4-6-0, despite its restrictive firebox capacity, was sufficient, with the quality of coal available, to provide the necessary power and adhesion for most express duties until the end of steam. The next logical step, to the 4-8-0, although proposed, was never taken.

● **BELOW**
Britain's Great Western Railway experimented with compounding in 1903 when Churchward introduced several engines on the De Glehn system. The first engine was built at Belfort, France, and named Le France. These compound Atlantics did not convince the Great Western to adopt the principle and they progressed to ultimate success with conventional 4-6-0s of two- and four-cylinder varieties.

PRINCESS CORONATION CLASS

Date	1937
Builder	Crewe Works, Cheshire, England
Client	London, Midland & Scottish Railway
Gauge	Standard
Driving wheels	6 ft 9 in
Capacity	4 cylinders 16 x 28 in
Total weight in full working order	165 tons

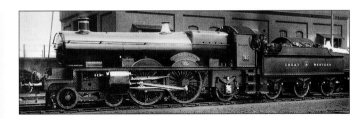

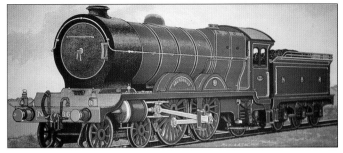

● **OPPOSITE**
William Stanier followed up his Princess Royal Pacifics with the Princess Coronations introduced in 1937. They hauled many of the heaviest trains on Britain's West Coast route until the end of steam.

● **ABOVE**
One of W.P. Read's Atlantics. These were the largest engines built for the North British Railway. They were introduced in 1906 and given Scottish names such as Aberdonian, Waverley and Highland Chief. They worked on the North British main lines, especially on the heavily graded Waverley route between Edinburgh and Carlisle in Cumbria.

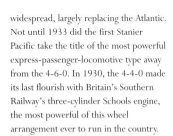

BRITISH MAIN-LINE LOCOMOTIVES – FREIGHT

● **BELOW**
Stanier's class 8F 2-8-0s were freight engines
and provided Britain's LMS with a robust
heavyfreight locomotive. They were a huge
advance on the 0-6-0 and 0-8-0 types.

The freight locomotive's evolution was less dramatic than that of its express passenger-hauling counterpart. The inside-cylinder 0-6-0s and 0-8-0s so prolific in the late-19th century continued to be built into the 20th century, although a major advance occurred in 1903 when Churchward introduced his 2800 class 2-8-0s. The 2-8-0 was pre-eminent until the end of steam. Churchward's engines were followed by Robinson's 04s for the Great Central Railway in 1911. Two years later, the 2-8-0 was taken up by Gresley on the Great Northern Railway. The London, Midland and Scottish (LMS) built most 2-8-0s: Stanier's 8Fs for LMS totalled 772 locomotives.

The modest size of British freight engines was given a massive boost in 1927 when the LMS introduced its 2-6-6-2T Garratts. These were built by Beyer Peacock of Manchester, northern England, to alleviate the double-heading of inside-cylinder 0-6-0s on Britain's Midland main line. Of these four-cylinder giants, 33 went into operation and demonstrated a potency hitherto

unknown on Britain's railways. Gresley turned to the 2-8-2 with his P1s of 1925. Two of these giants were built and hauled coal-trains weighing upwards of 2,000 tons.

The 2-8-2 was the next logical phase of development; as compared with the 2-10-1, it readily provided for a deep firebox with adequate space for the ashpan. Sadly, however, no further heavyfreight hauling 2-8-2s were ever built for use on the home railway, and the ultimate in British freight locomotives

● **BELOW LEFT**
Britain's first 2-10-0s were built for the Ministry of Supply in World War II by the North British works in Glasgow. With their more numerous 2-8-0 counterparts, they served in many countries during the war. The example shown here was taken into the stock of Greek State Railways.

● **BELOW RIGHT**
Gresley's V2 2-6-2 Green Arrow was one of the most successful classes in British locomotive history. They were true mixed-traffic engines capable of enormous haulage. They did monumental service in World War II and were popularly known in Britain as "the engines which won the war". Here, one is seen on the rollers of the British locomotive-testing plant at Swindon, Wiltshire.

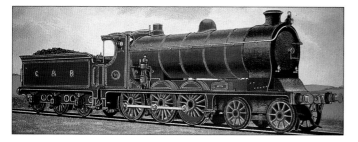

was the 2-10-0. This was not truly established until the 1950s, under the British Railways (BR) standard locomotive scheme. The 2-10-0s had first appeared as an Austerity version of the World War II 2-8-0s used for military operations, but these were primarily for light-axle loadings rather than sustained heavy haulage. The BR 9Fs were mineral haulers in their own right and building continued until 1960. An engine of this design became the last main-line locomotive built for Britain. It was named Evening Star. The 9Fs had a very short life for by 1968 steam operation in Britain ceased. They went to the scrapyard with all earlier forms of British freight locomotives – inside-cylinder 0-6-0s and 0-8-0s and the main 2-8-0 types.

LMS GARRATT

Date	1927
Builder	Beyer Peacock, Manchester, England
Client	London, Midland & Scottish Railway
Gauge	Standard
Driving wheels	5 ft 3 in
Capacity	4 cylinders 18 x 26 in
Steam pressure	190 lb sq in
Total weight in full working order	156 tons
Tractive effort	45,620 lbs

● **ABOVE LEFT**
The inside-cylinder 4-6-0 appeared on Scotland's Caledonian Railway in 1902. Over the next 12 years, the company's chief mechanical engineer (CME) J. F. McIntosh produced six different designs totalling 42 locomotives.

● **ABOVE RIGHT**
One of Churchward's 2800-class 2-8-0s introduced in 1903. The design caused his successor, Collett, to produce more between 1938-42 with only slight variations. Very few classes in British locomotive history have been built over a period as long as 40 years.

● **BELOW**
The LMS Garratt was a most exciting development in British freight-locomotive history. The engines were built for the LMS by Beyer Peacock. The class totalled 33 engines and hauled coal-trains over the Midland main line between Toton (Nottingham) and Cricklewood (north London). They took the place of two inside-cylinder 0-6-0s.

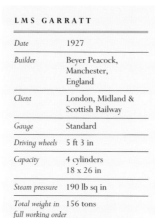

BRITISH SHUNTERS AND INDUSTRIAL LOCOMOTIVES

The traditional main-line shunting tank has been either an 0-4-0 or, more commonly, an 0-6-0. Numerous designs were created, especially Britain's LMS Jinty 0-6-0, of which more than 500 were built, and the Great Western 5700-class 0-6-0 pannier tanks, totalling 863 examples. Many more classes of 0-6-0 and even 0-8-0 tanks would have been built for shunting had not these forms of locomotives been heavily supplemented by downgraded inside-cylinder 0-6-0s and 0-8-0s. These engines, important main-line freight haulers in the closing years of the 19th century, became ideal heavy shunters and tripping engines in their

later years. Wagons had grown bigger, loads much heavier and the abundance of these downgraded freight engines meant the traditional 0-6-0 tank-engine did not evolve to any great size, remaining largely unchanged for almost a century.

Some larger marshalling yards – especially those with humps – needed something bigger than the 0-6-0, so special designs evolved to fill this niche. The first of these giants appeared in 1907 when John George Robinson introduced a three-cylinder 0-8-4T for humping at the Great Central Railway's Wath Yards, in the North Riding of Yorkshire. Two years later, the ever-prolific Wilson

Worsdell, CME of the North Eastern Railway, put into traffic some three-cylinder 4-8-0Ts. The LNWR introduced the first 30 0-8-2Ts in 1911, followed by 30 0-8-4Ts. These two classes were, in effect, a heavy tank-engine version of their standard 0-8-0 freight engines.

The definitive industrial locomotive evolved as either a side or saddle tank, four- or six-coupled. Larger industrial locomotives invariably came in the form of former main-line engines, which had been sold out of service. This practice led to tender-engines appearing on industrial lines. These environments often gave a massive extension of life to engines that

GWR 5700 CLASS	
Date	1929
Builder	Swindon Works, Wiltshire, England
Client	Great Western Railway
Gauge	Standard
Driving wheels	4 ft 7 in
Capacity	2 cylinders 17 x 24 in
Steam pressure	200 lb sq in
Total weight in full working order	51 tons
Tractive effort	2,255 lbs

● LEFT
Britain's Great Western Railway adopted the pannier tank for shunting operations. GWR's ultimate design was Collett's 5700-class with 4 ft 7 in wheels. Between 1929-49, 863 engines were built. When building ended, they were the largest class in Britain.

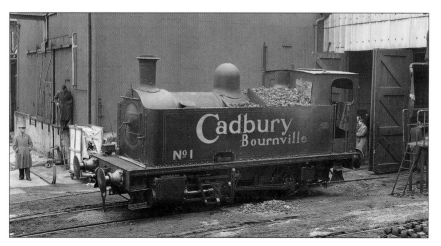

● **LEFT**
Worldwide, anywhere that was anywhere had steam railways. The steam locomotive was the prime source of motive power for all facets of industry. In Britain, typical of the diversity of the locomotive's locations was the railway network at Cadbury's chocolate-factory.

● **BELOW LEFT**
Andrew Barclay & Son, locomotive builders of Kilmarnock, Strathclyde, south-west Scotland, were famous for a long range of 0-4-0 and 0-6-0 saddle-tanks, which formed a distinctive family of engines built almost unchanged over a 70-year period. Here, one of their 0-4-0s works on the Storefield Ironstone system in Northamptonshire, in the English Midlands, taking iron ore to the connection with British Railways' main line.

had outlived their normal life span on main lines.

The basic industrial engine changed little in its century of pre-eminence. One fascinating variation, however, occurred in the form of the Fireless, of which some 200 worked in Britain. These engines were a low-cost shunting unit for industries with a ready supply of high-pressure steam. They took their steam secondhand from the works' boilers.

Up until World War II, several thousand industrial engines were active the length and breadth of Britain. Many survived in their industrial habitats after main-line steam working ended in 1968. This was historically appropriate. The world's first steam locomotive, created in a South Wales ironworks in 1804, was an industrial.

● **BELOW LEFT**
Britain's LMS Jinty 0-6-0s represented the ultimate manifestation of a long line of Midland Railway 0-6-0 shunting-tanks. They were found all over the English part of the LMS system in the years before most freight carriage was transferred from rail to road.

● **BELOW RIGHT**
Andrew Barclay pioneered the Fireless type in Britain and built many examples, both 0-4-0 and 0-6-0, for industrial establishments. The Fireless was arguably the most efficient and economical shunting unit ever devised.

BRITISH MAIN-LINE TANK ENGINES

The engines that worked suburban trains around Britain's great cities and conurbations were almost exclusively tank designs. The absence of a tender facilitated ease of running in either direction and cut out cumbersome and time-consuming turning. Also, the water's weight above the coupled wheels provided adhesion useful for rapid starts from stations. For similar reasons, tank-engines were favoured on branch lines across Britain.

In the 19th century, the urban and branch-line tank-engine evolved in many forms: 2-4-0, 4-4-0, 4-4-2, 0-4-2, 0-4-4 and 0-6-0.

The 0-4-4 was particularly favoured. It had flexibility to run in either direction. Its boiler and cylinder blocks were often interchangeable with sister inside-cylinder 0-6-0s and inside-cylinder 4-4-0 express-passenger engines.

● **LEFT**
Britain's London and North Western Railway used many tank engines on suburban and branch lines, particularly 0-6-2 and 2-4-2 types. For faster intermediate work, Bowen Cooke introduced this class of 4-6-2 superheated tank engine.

As the population of Britain's cities grew, so did the suburban tank's proportions. It graduated to the 4-4-2 and by the turn of the century, with the harmonious 4-4-4, in sheer aesthetic terms, reached its pièce de résistance, the ultimate in balanced proportions.

The most remarkable suburban engine was Holden's Decapod 0-10-0T for the Great Eastern Railway (GER). Advocates of electrification claimed that a 315-ton train could be accelerated to 30 mph in 30 seconds. Holden, in producing his Decapod, proved that this achievement could be bettered with steam. As a result, the proposed electrification of GER's suburban services from London's Liverpool Street Station was shelved.

● **BELOW**
An 0-6-0 shunting-tank of Britain's North Eastern Railway, from a class of 120 engines built between 1886–95. The type's suitability is shown by the introduction of a second and similar batch in 1898 of which 85 were built by 1925. Then, 28 more were built between 1949–51, under British Railways. This created the unique situation of a design being built over a 54-year period. Possibly no other class in world locomotive history has achieved this distinction.

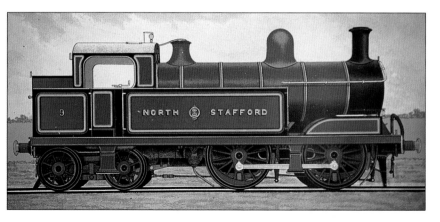

● **LEFT**
The 0-4-4 T's flexibility
was shown by this
example from
England's North
Staffordshire Railway.
Classified as "M", five
examples of the type
were built in 1907–8.

● **BELOW**
Britain's Great Western
Railway (GWR)
achieved excellent
standardization in all
categories of motive
power. For suburban
and branch-line work,
Churchward
introduced a range
of 2-6-2s.

Alas, the Decapod was so heavy on the track that it never entered service.

Six-coupled engines in the form of 0-6-2s and 0-6-4s progressed to 2-6-2s and 2-6-4s, the preferred power from the 1930s onwards. Many of these engines were mixed-traffic types, equally suited for cross-country and branch-line work as well.

Electrification – especially of metropolitan and suburban services – progressively eroded the need for tank engines, particularly on Britain's Southern Railway. A partial erosion of need also occurred on branch lines, where demoted express-passenger designs of earlier years were used, 2-4-0s and 4-4-0s being especially common.

The tank-engine is popularly thought of as something of a plodding machine. In truth, many were extremely fast runners, and speeds of 70 mph were quite normal on many suburban and outer-suburban workings, some of which were very tightly timed and had to be fitted in between the paths of more important, longer-distance trains.

● **BELOW**
This engine belonged to a class of Ivatt 0-6-2Ts with 5 ft 8 in wheels, built for the Great Northern Railway (GNR) between 1906–12. The class totalled 56 engines. These appeared prolifically on suburban workings out of London's Kings Cross Station. Many had condensing apparatus for working through metropolitan tunnels. In their later years, many were found on suburban workings around Leeds and Bradford, in west Yorkshire.

LNER CLASS J72
0-6-0T

Date	1898
Builder	Darlington Locomotive Works, Co. Durham, England
Client	North Eastern Railway; London & North Eastern Railway; British Railways
Gauge	4 ft 8 in
Driving wheels	4 ft 1 in
Capacity	2 cylinders 17 x 24 in
Steam pressure	140 lb sq in
Weight	43 tons
Tractive effort	16,760 lbs

BRITISH EXPORTS

The steam-locomotive was arguably Britain's greatest technological contribution to mankind. Her lead in railways ensured wide opportunities, and she became railway builder to her empire and the world. A vast locomotive industry developed quite separately from that of the famous railway towns, which served Britain's domestic needs. Legendary foundries in Glasgow, Scotland, and in the English provinces at Leeds in Yorkshire, Newcastle upon Tyne in Northumberland (now Tyne and Wear), Darlington in Durham, Manchester and other parts of Lancashire, and in Stafford, west central England, sent

● **LEFT**
Manning Wardle of Leeds, west Yorkshire, built this Crane Tank locomotive in 1903. It lifted tree trunks at an Indian sawmill, replacing elephants.

locomotives worldwide, often exporting the industrial revolution with them. Lands beyond the British Empire were served, including those having no political affinity with Britain. Exported locomotives reflected the designs of engines running in the mother country, and the types of engines seen rolling through the soft English countryside

were soon found crossing barren, rugged and jungle-clad landscapes in many countries of Africa, Australia, South-east Asia and South America.

Britain's role as locomotive-builder to the world remained largely unchallenged throughout the 19th century, but the early 20th saw serious competition for the first time, especially from America and, to a lesser extent, from builders in continental Europe. America's engines were a commercial threat and also challenged conventional British design. These, though produced by skilled craftsmen, nonetheless had deficiencies. These, not apparent in Britain, caused problems in the rough-and-tumble of world railways.

● **LEFT**
The lineage of these British build Pacifics is fully shown in this scene of a South African Railways 3 ft 6 in gauge 16CR heading over flood waters of the tidal Swartkops River in Port Elizabeth, Cape Province, South Africa.

● **RIGHT**
One of a group of Moguls built in 1899 by Beyer Peacock of Manchester, Lancashire, for Brazil's Leopoldina Railway. This Mogul is an example of exported types being used abroad before coming into service in the country of manufacture.

● **RIGHT**
In East Africa, the scrublands of Tanzania resounded to the wail of British locomotives in the 1920s after the territory was mandated to Britain at the end of World War I, when it was known as Tanganyika. This light-axle 2-8-2 was ideal for riding the lightly laid and rough track beds common in Africa.

BAGNALL 2-8-2

Date	1947
Builder	Bagnall's of Stafford, Staffordshire, England
Client	Tanganyika Railway, East Africa
Gauge	Metre
Driving wheels	3 ft 7 in
Capacity	Cylinders 17 x 23 in
Steam pressure	180 lb sq in
Total weight full working order	100 tons
Tractive effort	25,050 lb

Most British locomotives had small fireboxes set between the frames, a restriction that caused steaming difficulties when inferior coal was used.

Traditional British plate frames gave problems when engines ran on the developing world's poor quality tracks. American engines had wide fireboxes suitable for inferior fuel. Their bar-frames enjoyed greater tolerance in adverse conditions. Some British loco-motives' limited bearing surfaces also gave trouble in rough conditions.

American engines' bearing proportions were more generous.

An immediate effect of America's aggressive export drive in the early 20th century was the amalgamation in 1903 of Glasgow's three big builders – Sharp Stewart, Neilson and Dübs – to form the North British Locomotive Company. Although there was a shift towards a more international design of locomotive, created in the light of world experience, British builders retained a significant role right to the end of the steam age.

● **RIGHT**

Britain's private loco-motive builders often built for companies in Britain whose works were unable to supply engines quickly enough. Here, at the North British Works in Glasgow, Scotland, an LNER class B1 4-6-0 is in the background, by a light-axle loaded 2-8-2 for East African Railways.

BRITISH RECORD-BREAKERS AND STREAMLINERS

The commonly held view that the steam-locomotive was replaced because it was slow is incorrect. Many of today's diesel and even electrically operated services are not appreciably faster than steam was 50 or more years ago.

The magical three-figure speed was reached in 1903 by the Great Western Railway's 4-4-0 City of Truro. This achieved 102.3 mph down Wellington Bank in Somerset, south-west England, with an Ocean Mails train, the first time any form of transport reached 100 mph.

GWR featured in another speed dash, with a Churchward Saint Class 4-6-0, which allegedly reached 120 mph while running light engine on a test trip after an overhaul at Swindon works in Wiltshire. This alleged achievement is not authenticated, but over the years authorities have claimed it to be true.

The 1930s, the "streamlined era", were a time of epic record-breaking runs all over the world. Streamlining was in vogue. It inspired and fascinated the public, but its usefulness in reaching high speeds was soon questioned.

The legendary speed records of the

LNER A4 PACIFIC	
Date	1935
Builder	Doncaster Works, south Yorkshire
Client	London & North Eastern Railway
Gauge	Standard
Driving wheels	6 ft 8 in
Capacity	3 cylinders 18 x 26 in
Total weight in full working order	167 tons
Steam pressure	250 lb sq in
Tractive effort	33,455 lb

● BELOW
Great Western Railway's Castles were distinguished among British express-passenger designs. They first appeared in 1923. Their exploits on the Cheltenham Flyer were legendary, and for some years the Flyer was the world's fastest train. In 1924 the engine shown, No. 4079 Pendennis Castle, running from Paddington, London, to Plymouth, Devon, averaged 60 mph between Paddington and Westbury, Wiltshire, with a 530-tonne train.

● LEFT
The LNER's plaque affixed to the boiler of Mallard to commemorate its world record-breaking run in 1938.

● BELOW
The LNER class-A4 No.4468 Mallard, dubbed the world's fastest steam locomotive. Mallard's record may remain unbeaten.

● BELOW
The Princess Royals were followed by the Princess Coronations. One of these engines, streamlined, briefly held the world record for steam traction of 114 mph. Over the years after World War II, all streamlined examples lost their casing.

● ABOVE
Stanier's record-breaking Princess Royal Pacific No. 6201 Princess Elizabeth, which in 1936 covered the 401 miles between Glasgow, Scotland, and London Euston in 5 hours 44 minutes – an average speed of 70 mph. Almost 60 years later, in November 1996, the *Daily Telegraph* reported that many electrically operated services on the West Coast route were slower than Princess Elizabeth's epic run.

1930s were again the result of competition between the East and West Coast routes linking London and Scotland. Both the LMS and the LNER had brand new designs of Pacific locomotives in service – streamlined Coronations on the former and Gresley A4s on the latter.

In terms of maximum speed, the LMS bid for the world speed record on 29 June 1937 when a special run of the Coronation Scot was made for the press six days before the service's official start. The locomotive, No. 6220 Coronation, reached 114 mph down Madeley Bank on the approaches to Crewe, Cheshire, in northern England. Alas, the bank was not long enough and the train was still doing 60-70 mph when the platform signal came into sight and rapid braking for a standstill in Crewe Station smashed all the crockery in the dining car.

The LNER would not countenance the LMS taking the honour in this way. Almost a year later, on 3 July 1938, the A4 class Pacific Mallard, ostensibly on a special run to test braking, achieved 126 mph on the descent of Stoke Bank, between Grantham in Lincolnshire and Peterborough in Cambridgeshire, eastern England, thus beating the LMS and setting a never-beaten world speed record for the steam locomotive.

Non-streamlined activity in the 1930s was also exciting, not least with the Cheltenham Flyer express, which was booked to run the 77.3 miles from Paddington, London, to Swindon, Wiltshire, in 65 minutes. On one occasion the distance was covered in 56 minutes. This involved a start-to-stop average of 82 mph.

World War II ended any such performances and in the postwar period the railway network's recovery was slow. Not until the 1950s did three-figure speeds with steam reappear.

AMERICAN MIKADOS

The 2-8-2 Mikado-type locomotive was developed in 1897 for Japanese Railways by the Baldwin Locomotive Works, the largest and most prolific locomotive-builder in the United States of America.

● LEFT
Denver & Rio Grande Western used several classes of 36 in gauge Mikados on its narrow-gauge lines in Colorado. A K36 and larger K37 are seen at Chama, New Mexico. The K37s were rebuilt from standard-gauge locomotives.

● **AN AMERICAN ENGINE FOR JAPAN**
The Mikado-type locomotive derives its name from this first owner, though during World War II, when America was fighting Japan, American nationalists tried to change the name to "MacArthur-type". Many Americans call these locomotives "Mikes".

In 1905, the Northern Pacific Railway was the first railroad to embrace the Mikado in large numbers. The locomotive quickly caught on, and many were produced for many railroads until about 1930. Some 10,000 were built for domestic use, and more than 4,000 were built for export.

● **A SOLID DESIGN**
The 2-8-2 wheel arrangement was a natural progression from the popular 2-8-0 Consolidation-type and 2-6-2 Prairie-type. The Mikado's overall design was outstanding. It was well balanced, providing excellent tractive effort and a good ride. The trailing truck allowed for a larger firebox, therefore more steam capacity and larger cylinders, giving the engine greater power than earlier designs which it rendered obsolete. When technological advances such as superheating were developed, they were used on the Mikado to great success. The

locomotive's primary application was heavy freight service, though many railroads used lighter Mikes on branch lines.

● **NARROW-GAUGE APPLICATION**
The Mikado type was particularly well adapted to narrow-gauge freight service because of its balanced design and four sets of drivers. These provided the traction needed on heavy mountain grades, while producing only minimum wear and tear on lightweight track and right-of-way. In the West, Denver & Rio Grande Western (D&RGW) operated four classes of Mikado on its rugged mountain grades. Its

● LEFT
Saginaw Timber No. 2 is a light Mikado typically used on short lines for hauling freight and passengers.

● **LEFT**
Pennsylvania
Railroad (PRR)
No. 1596, a Class-
L1s Mikado-type,
features a boxy
Belpaire-type
firebox, standard on
most late-era PRR
steam locomotives.
It is pictured near
the end of its active
life, at Enola,
Pennsylvania.

line over the 3,048 m (10,003 ft) high Cumbres Pass, in the San Juan Mountains of south Colorado, featured gruelling 4 per cent grades, which gave the 3 ft narrow-gauge Mikado a real proving ground. In the East, narrow-gauge coal hauler East Broad Top also preferred the Mikados, owning several from Baldwin. Many of these narrow-gauge locomotives are preserved in working order.

MISSOURI PACIFIC MIKADO TYPE	
Date	1923
Builder	American Locomotive Co. (Alco)
Client	Missouri Pacific
Gauge	4 ft 8½ in
Driving wheels	65 in
Capacity	2 cylinders 27 x 32 in
Steam pressure	200 lb
Weight	305,115 lb
Tractive effort	62,950 lb

● **RIGHT**
The Duluth &
Northern
Minnesota's Mikado
No. 14 clips along
north of Duluth,
Minnesota. This
light Mikado was
built by Baldwin in
1913.

● **RIGHT**
This 2-8-2 Mikado-
type was built by the
American
Locomotive
Company (Alco) at
its Brooks Works in
1920. It worked for
the Aberdeen &
Rockfish Railroad,
and serves the Valley
Railroad at Essex,
Connecticut, New
Maryland.

AMERICAN ARTICULATED LOCOMOTIVES

The Mallet-type compound articulated steam locomotive, named after Swiss inventor Anatole Mallet, had been popular in Europe for decades before its eventual introduction in the United States of America.

● B&O EMPLOYS THE MALLET

After the turn of the century, a need for greater tractive effort led American railroads to employ articulated steam locomotives with two sets of driving wheels. The compound articulated

BALTIMORE & OHIO MALLET-TYPE NO. 2400 "OLD MAUD"	
Date	1904
Builder	American Locomotive Co. (Alco)
Client	Baltimore & Ohio Railroad
Gauge	4 ft 8½ in
Driving wheels	56 in
Capacity	4 cylinders: 2 (20 x 32 in) and 2 (32 x 32 in)
Steam pressure	235 lb
Weight	334,500 lb
Tractive effort	71,500 lb

The Baltimore & Ohio's articulated 2-8-8-2 Class KK1 was an experimental locomotive that featured a water-tube boiler (most American locomotives had fire-tube boilers). It delivered a 90,000 lb tractive effort.

● LEFT
Union Pacific (UP) 4-6-6-4 Challenger-type simple articulated No. 3985 at Portola, California. UP owned more than 100 locomotives of this type for heavy-freight service in western USA.

engine reused steam from high-pressure cylinders, in low-pressure cylinders, to achieve maximum efficiency. On most Mallets, very large low-pressure cylinders were used at the first set of drivers, while high-pressure cylinders were used at the second.

In 1904, the American Locomotive Company (Alco) built the first American Mallet-type, a 0-6-6-0 compound articulated nicknamed "Old Maud", for the Baltimore & Ohio Railroad (B&O), a

coalhauler facing many steep grades. While Mallet-types were effective for slow-speed service, few railroads used them for general service on the main line.

● THE SIMPLE ARTICULATED GAINS POPULARITY

The articulated concept achieved greater popularity in a more traditional format. This was the simple articulated engine, which has two sets of cylinders but does not reuse steam. Most articulated engines

● LEFT
The Baltimore & Ohio's No. 2400 was the first American locomotive to use the Mallet design. It was built in 1904 by Alco and widely known as "Old Maud". It weighed 334,500 lb and had a 71,500 lb tractive effort.

built after about 1910 were not compounds and thus not true Mallets. While many railroads preferred simple articulated engines, the Norfolk & Western (N&WR) continued to perfect the Mallet. The N&WR class-Y6b built by the railroad's Roanoke shops in North

Carolina for main-line service represented the zenith of the type. N&WR was one of the last American railroads to use Mallets in regular main-line service.

The development of articulated steam locomotives, combined with other improvements such as mechanical stokers and superheaters, eventually led to the building of the world's largest locomotives. Among the largest articulateds were the 2-8-8-4 Yellowstone type used by Northern Pacific and ore-hauler Duluth, Missabi & Iron Range (DM&IR); the 2-6-6-6 Allegheny type built by the Lima Locomotive works for the Chesapeake & Ohio and Virginian Railway, in 1941 and 1945 respectively; and the 4-8-8-4 Big Boy type built for Union Pacific lines between 1941–44.

● **SOUTHERN PACIFIC CAB FORWARD**

The Southern Pacific (SP) developed a unique variation of the articulated engine. The traditional steam locomotive configuration featuring the cab behind the boiler proved unsatisfactory on the big articulateds when operating in the long tunnels and snowsheds found on the 2,174 metre (7,135 ft) Donner Pass in California's Sierra Nevada. Crews suffered from smoke inhalation. So SP turned the engine around, placing the cab in front of the boiler. The first of SP's 256 cab-forward articulated was a Mallet-type built in 1910. The last were Baldwin-built articulated 2-8-8-4 types, the SP class-AC-12, built in 1944.

● **ABOVE**
Among the heaviest articulated steam locomotives ever built were 2-8-8-4 Yellowstone types made for Northern Pacific (NP) and Duluth, Missabi & Iron Range (DM&IR).

● **RIGHT**
Norfolk & Western continued to perfect the Mallet compound-articulated-locomotive design long after other railroads adopted the simple articulated. An N&WR Y6 Mallet 2-8-8-2 pictured near Blue Ridge Summit, West Virginia, in 1958.

AMERICAN PACIFICS

The 4-6-2 Pacific-type steam locomotive came into favour shortly after the turn of the century and was produced widely for many American railroads until the 1930s.

● PREMIER PASSENGER POWER

This locomotive followed the logical developmental progression from the 4-4-0 American-type, 4-4-2 Atlantic-type and, to a lesser extent, the 2-6-2 Prairie-type. Most Pacifics, designed for high-speed passenger service, had relatively large fireboxes and high drivers. By 1915, this type had supplanted 4-6-0 Ten Wheelers and 4-4-2 Atlantics on crack passenger-trains. All around America, flashy high-drivered Pacifics were hauling name trains. These included Northern Pacific's luxurious North Coast Limited, Southern Pacific's Sunset Limited and the Pennsylvania Railroad's Broadway Limited.

● **BELOW**
The Baltimore & Ohio's Pacific type, No. 5305.

● **OPPOSITE TOP**
The Louisville & Nashville's Pacific-type No. 152 was built by Alco's Rogers Works in January 1905. This locomotive served the railroad for nearly 50 years.

● THE PACIFIC ADAPTS WELL TO NEW TECHNOLOGY AND STYLES

The Pacific-type was well suited to technological improvements. Superheating, mechanical stokers and roller bearings were developed. Superheating recirculated hot steam through the engine's firetubes, allowing for more power and greater efficiency. These developments were applied to both new and existing Pacifics, dramatically improving the performance of the engines. In the 1930s, when streamlined trains became the latest thing in railroad style, some railroads dressed up their Pacifics in snazzy shrouds.

● PENNSYLVANIA RAILROAD K4

The best-known, most loved and perhaps the best-performing Pacific was the Pennsylvania Railroad's Class K4. PPR received its first Pacific-type from Alco in 1907, an experimental locomotive Class K28. This locomotive led to several other

classes of Pacific, with the culmination of design exhibited in the 1914 Class K4. A masterpiece of engineering, the K4 was an outstanding performer. Eventually, Pennsylvania rostered some 425 K4s, an exceptional number for a single class of locomotive. They were the railroad's preferred passenger locomotive for nearly 30 years. Some K4s were built by Baldwin but many were constructed at the railroad's Juniata Shops. Like many PRR steam locomotives, the K4 featured the boxy Belpaire-type firebox. The last K4 was retired from regular service in 1957.

● **LEFT**
The Southern Pacific's No. 2472 was one of 15 Class-P8 Pacific types in the railroad's passenger fleet. These 1912 Baldwin-built locomotives had a 43,660-lb tractive effort.

● **ABOVE**
A highly polished Pennsylvania Railroad K4 Pacific, No. 5475.

PENNSYLVANIA RAILROAD K4 PACIFIC

Date	1914 –28
Builder	Juniata Shops, Baldwin, Pennsylvania, USA
Client	Pennsylvania Railroad
Gauge	4 ft 8½ in
Driving wheels	80 in
Capacity	2 cylinders 27 x 28 in
Steam pressure	205 lb
Weight	468,000 lb
Tractive effort	44,460 lb

SHAYS AND SWITCHERS

American logging railroads had special locomotive requirements because their track, often crudely built, used very sharp curves and negotiated grades as steep as 10 per cent. Also, these railroads required locomotives that could haul relatively heavy loads at very slow speeds.

● SHAYS AND OTHER GEARED LOCOMOTIVES

To meet these requirements, three builders specialized in constructing flexible, high-adhesion steam locomotives that operated with a geared drive, rather than the direct drive used on conventional locomotives. These builders were Lima, at Ohio, with the Shay-type; Heisler Locomotive Works, at Eire, Pennsylvania, and Climax Locomotive and Machine Works at Corry, Pennsylvania. Each builder used the same basic principle – a cylinder-driven shaft that connected to the driving wheels using bevelled gears – but each approached the concept slightly differently.

● ABOVE
This is a stock Shay, built by Lima in 1928. It was sold to the Mayo Lumber Company and operated in British Columbia, Canada. It is preserved, with other Shays, at the Cass Scenic Railroad, West Virginia, USA.

Lima's Shay was the most popular type. It used a row of vertical cylinders on the fireman's side, that is the right-hand side of the engine, to power a shaft that connected two or three sets of driving wheels. Two-cylinder Shays had two sets of driving wheels; three-cylinder Shays had three sets of driving wheels. The Shay-type was first constructed in the 1880s.

Heisler used two cylinders facing one another crosswise, one on each side of the locomotive, forming a V-pattern. These cylinders turned a shaft to power two sets of driving wheels. Climax used two parallel, sharply inclined cylinders, one on each side of the locomotive, to power a shaft connecting two sets of driving wheels.

● SWITCHERS

Most railroads used specialized locomotives of a conventional design for switching service at yards, terminals and industrial sites. Because most switchers were relatively small locomotives, operated at slow speeds, and needed high adhesion to move long cuts of cars, they normally did not have pilot or trailing trucks – commonly used on road locomotives.

The smallest switchers were 0-4-0 types. This sort of locomotive, however,

had low adhesion and a notoriously bad-ride quality, so locomotives with more driving wheels were generally preferred. The 0-6-0 switcher was the most popular for general switching and about 10,000 were built. Some railroads used 0-8-0 switchers for heavier switching duties and, after the turn of the century, 0-10-0 switchers saw only limited service in hump yards.

Specialty tenderless switchers, with water-tanks built over the boilers, and "fireless" steam engines saw limited use in areas where conventional locomotives were inappropriate.

TYPICAL 0-6-0 SWITCHER	
Date	About 1905
Builder	American Locomotive Co. (Alco)
Gauge	4 ft 8½ in
Driving wheels	51 in
Capacity	2 cylinders 19 x 24 in
Steam pressure	180 lb
Weight	163,365 lb
Tractive effort	26,510 lb

● **OPPOSITE**
Heisler's geared locomotives use two cylinders in a V position. This Heisler was built in 1912 for the Louise Lumber Company of Hawkes, Mississippi. It operates on the Silver Creek & Stephenson Railroad in Freeport, Illinois, USA.

● **RIGHT**
The last of the Lima-built Shay-types were heavy, three-cylinder locomotives built in 1945. The Western Maryland railroad in the USA owned several of these big Shays. They weighed 324,000 lb and generated a 59,740 lb tractive effort.

● **ABOVE**
Locomotive 2-8-0, No. 207 (formerly Southern 630), and North American Rayon Company's fireless 0-6-0T, No. 1, on the East Tennessee and Western North Carolina Railroad, USA.

● **BELOW**
Surrounded by lumber, this Ely Thomas Lumber Company's Lima-built Shay-type No. 2 waits for its next run in 1958 near Gauley, West Virginia, USA.

AMERICAN EXPORTS

Nations around the world relied on the locomotive prowess of the United States of America to supply their motive-power needs. Of some 175,000 steam locomotives built in the USA in the 120 years between 1830 and 1950, about 37,000, more than 20 per cent, were built specifically for export. Many varieties of locomotives were sold, depending on customers' needs, but five types were particularly popular in the export market and represented the lion's share of those sold.

● CONSOLIDATIONS

The most popular export model was the 2-8-0 Consolidation. More than 10,000 were sold outside the USA. This model was the second most-popular domestic locomotive, too. More than 22,000 were built for use in the USA where only the 19th-century 4-4-0 American-type was more popular.

A distant second to the Consolidation was the 2-8-2 Mikado-type. More than 4,000 were exported. This type was specifically designed by Baldwin

Locomotive Works for Japanese Railways in 1897. Later, it was adapted for domestic use. Many were used for freight service in the USA.

● DECAPODS FOR RUSSIA

The 2-10-0 Decapod was the third most-popular model. Many of the heavy locomotives went to Russia and to the Soviet Union during World Wars I and II. The Decapod was also popular in Germany, Greece, Poland and Turkey. Oddly, it was not very popular in the

MACARTHUR 2-8-2 USATC	
Builder	Baldwin Locomotive Company, Eddystone, Pennsylvania, USA
Client	United States Army Transport Corps (USATC)
Gauge	Metre
Driving wheels	4 ft
Capacity	Cylinders 16 x 24 in
Weight in full working order	112 tons

● LEFT

One of the last surviving MacArthur 2-8-2s. These metre-gauge engines were built for the United States Army Transport Corps (USATC) for operations during World War II. They saw wide service in India, Burma, Thailand and the Philippines. After the war, survivors remained active. In India, they were classified MAWD (McArthur War Department) and found in the country's Northeast Frontier region.

● ABOVE
Cuba's Manuel Isla sugar mill is host to this vintage Baldwin 0-4-2 tank believed to have been built in 1882. A retired employee at the mill, 88-year-old Jose Alfonso Melgoragio, remembers knowing the engine all his life. He worked on it for 25 years.

● LEFT
This classic American ten-wheeler, built by Rogers of New Jersey in 1896, pictured at the San Barnado Locomotive Works near Santiago, Chile, where the veteran was ending its days as work's pilot.

● ABOVE LEFT
A night scene in the mountains of the Philippines island of Negros. Two last survivors of their respective types are seen at the Insula Lumber Company. On the left, a Baldwin-built, four-cylinder compound Mallet; on the right, a vertical-cylinder Shay. These are classic American locomotives of the American Pacific Northwest.

● LEFT
A rare Baldwin 2-6-2 saddle-tank, known as the "Lavras Rose", which as Baldwin export order No. 372 of 1927 operated as a work's shunter at Lavras in Mina Gerais State, Brazil.

domestic market. Only the Santa Fe and Pennsylvania Railroad owned large numbers. The Frisco picked up Decapods intended for Russia and used them successfully for many years. Of the 4,100 American-built Decapods, 3,400 were exported around the world.

● EXPORTS OF MOGULS AND TEN-WHEELERS
Nearly 3,000 2-6-0 Mogul-types were built for export. This locomotive was popular for heavy freight in the mid-19th century. Some 1,600 4-6-0 ten-wheeler types were also exported, nearly 10 per cent of American production. Of 3,800 geared locomotives built in the USA for use on steep grades and for specialty railroads, such as logging, 600 were exported.

● BELOW LEFT
This classic American switcher once worked for the 5 ft 3 in gauge Paulista Railway serving the city and Pernambuco state in eastern Brazil. It was built by Baldwin of Philadelphia, Pennsylvania, USA, in 1896. The veteran is pictured here pensioned off to industrial service at the Cosim Steelworks at São Paulo, Brazil.

STREAMLINED STEAM

In 1934, at the height of the Great Depression, the Burlington railroad's Budd-built stainless-steel streamlined Pioneer Zephyr streaked across America.

● STREAMLINING TAKES OFF

Everywhere Pioneer Zephyr went, it inspired railroad managers and the riding public. In a similar vein, Union Pacific's streamlined City of Salina toured the West. These Winton engine-powered diesel articulated "trains of the future" soon resulted in the streamlining of a great many steam locomotives for passenger service. New locomotives, steam, diesel-electric and electric, were ordered as well, along with whole streamlined trains of luxurious passenger cars.

● DRESSING UP THE OLD GUARD

The railroads were quick to send crack passenger locomotives to shop for a fancy new dress. In 1936, Pennsylvania Railroad hired noted industrial designer

● BELOW
The Chesapeake & Ohio railroad operated four Class L1 streamlined 4-6-4 Hudson types in passenger service. These odd-looking, yellow and stainless-steel adorned locomotives were nicknamed "Yellowbellies".

Raymond Loewy to improve K4 No. 3768 aesthetically. The result was a flashy-looking locomotive. Many railroads dressed up their older locomotives with elaborate shrouding, though in some cases with less than superlative results. In many cases, shrouding hampered maintenance and was later removed.

● NEW STREAMLINERS

The Milwaukee Road was one of the first railroads to order new streamlined steam locomotives. In 1935, it ordered high-speed 4-4-2s with 84 in driving wheels and shrouds designed by Otto Kuhler. Assigned to its Hiawathas, these fast engines would regularly zip at more than 100 mph between Chicago, Illinois, and Milwaukee, Wisconsin.

Beginning in the late 1930s, Southern Pacific's fleet of semi-streamlined 4-8-4 Northern types, painted in its flashy orange, red and silver "Daylight" scheme, marched about California. The epitome of this famous class were the 30 GS-4s and GS-5s built by the Lima works in 1941–42. These powerful engines exhibited some of the finest styling found on any North American locomotive.

Among the last types of streamlined locomotive built were the Norfolk & Western's J Class 4-8-4s, for service with its passenger-trains.

● RIGHT
The Norfolk & Western Railroad's Class-J Northerns, Nos. 600 to 612, were its most famous streamliners. These powerful locomotives could operate to a top speed of 110 mph but rarely needed to. N&WR operated other streamline steam as well, including its 800 Series Class K-2, 4-8-2 Mountains. Two N&WR Js pause for servicing in 1958.

SOUTHERN PACIFIC GS-4	
Date	1941
Builder	Lima, Ohio, USA
Client	Southern Pacific
Gauge	4 ft 8½ in
Driving wheels	80 in
Capacity	2 cylinders 26 x 32 in
Steam pressure	300 lb
Weight	475,000 lb
Tractive effort	78,650 lb

● **ABOVE**
Canadian National Railway 4-8-4 No. 6402 passing through Toronto.

● **BELOW**
Southern Pacific owned a fleet of semi-streamlined, "Daylight"-painted 4-8-4 Northern types for fast passenger service. Of these, the best performing and most aesthetically pleasing were 30 Class GS-4s and GS-5s built in 1941–42.

THE NETWORK EXPANDS – DECAPODS, MOUNTAINS, SANTA FES AND OVERLANDS

The railroads of the United States of America had an insatiable appetite for ever-larger, more powerful and more efficient locomotives. It stemmed from their belief that more powerful locomotives would produce lower operating costs through the ability to haul more goods, faster, with fewer crews and locomotives.

In the 19th century, locomotive output was limited to the size of the firebox and the fireman's ability to shovel coal. Early attempts at producing big locomotives usually resulted in curious behemoths that did not steam well and languished for lack of power. The development of superheating (recirculation of steam through a locomotive's firetubes, significantly increasing power) and of the trailing truck (enabling an increase in firebox capacity) allowed for significant increases in practical locomotive size and for the development of several large new locomotive types. The further

development of devices such as the mechanical stoker (moving coal from tender to firebox without a shovel) allowed for maximum performance from new larger locomotives.

CHESAPEAKE & OHIO CLASS J1 MOUNTAIN TYPE

Date	1911–12
Builder	American Locomotive Co. (Alco)
Client	Chesapeake & Ohio Railroad
Gauge	4 ft 8½ in
Driving wheels	62 in
Capacity	2 cylinders 29 x 28 in
Steam pressure	180 lb
Weight	499,500 lb
Tractive effort	58,000 lb

● **DECAPOD AND MOUNTAIN-TYPES**

The 2-10-0 Decapod-type, first introduced in 1870 by the Lehigh Valley Railroad, Pennsylvania, proved too big for its time. After 1900, it was built with limited success for several American railroads. It was most successful in the export market.

The 4-8-2 was introduced in about 1910 for use on the Chesapeake & Ohio railroad and soon proved a very popular design. This versatile type of locomotive was well suited for fast passenger-trains.

● **SANTA FE AND OVERLAND-TYPES**

Western railroads, which operated over great distances across the open plains, mountains and deserts, had a special need for large, powerful locomotives and

● **ABOVE**
The 2-10-0 Decapod type was not popular among American railroads, but Pennsylvania Railroad owned more than 500. The Decapod was used for heavy, slow-speed freight service.

● **RIGHT**
The Norfolk & Western Railroad operated streamlined 4-8-2 Mountain types in passenger service. These locomotives, Class K2, looked very similar to the J Class Northern types.

were better able to handle those with a long wheelbase. Shortly after the turn of the century, the Santa Fe Railway took delivery of 2-10-2 locomotives called Santa Fe types. This type did not attain popularity with other railroads until World War I, when changes in technology made it more appealing and the type was mass produced. In the 1920s, the Union Pacific railroad took delivery of a three-cylinder 4-10-2 locomotive named after that railroad's primary corridor, the Overland Route. Southern Pacific also ordered this type and referred to it as the Southern Pacific type. The 4-10-2 was not very popular. Fewer than 100 were built.

● **ABOVE**
This Baltimore & Ohio railroad's 4-8-2 brand new Mountain type poses for its builder's photograph. This locomotive had 74 in driving wheels, 30 x 30 in cylinders, operated at 210 lb per sq in and produced a 65,000 lb tractive effort.

AMERICAN SUPERPOWER

American locomotive builders were constantly looking to improve the steam locomotives' output and fuel economy, and in doing so developed many important innovations.

● FOUR-AXLE TRAILING TRUCK KEY TO POWER

The development of the four-axle trailing-truck or -tender allowed for a larger firebox, and thus increased the heating surface and power. "Superpower" also took advantage of other improvements, such as automatic stokers, superheating and, later, roller bearings.

The first locomotive exhibiting the radial, outside-bearing, four-axle truck and enlarged firebox was a Lima 2-8-4 built in 1925 for the New York Central railroad. It was designed for heavyfreight service. NYC used its 2-8-4s on the Boston & Albany (B&A) line in western Massachusetts. This line featured the

steepest grades on NYC's system. As a result, this new type was named the "Berkshire", after the mountain range in which it operated. The Berkshire type was the logical progression from the Mikado type, long popular for freight service. NYC was pleased with the Berkshires' performance and ordered a fleet of them for service on the B&A line. There they served for more than 20 years, until the introduction of diesel-electric.

● SUPER PASSENGER POWER

The four-axle trailing-truck and larger firebox principle worked so well on the freight-hauling Berkshire that the same principle was tried on fast passenger locomotives. In 1927, NYC took delivery of its first 4-6-4 locomotive from Alco. This type was named after the Hudson River, NYC's famed Water Level Route, which runs parallel to the line between New York City and Albany, the state capital.

● **LEFT**
One of the most impressive types of steam locomotive ever built was Atchison, Topeka & Santa Fe's 2900 Series, 4-8-4 Northerns. They weighed 510,000 lb, operated at 300 lb per sq in and had 80 in driving wheels. They regularly ran at more than 100 miles an hour.

● **OPPOSITE**
In 1945, Reading Railroad built eight 4-8-4
Northerns, Class T1, at its shops in Reading,
Pennsylvania. Designed for freight service, the
T1 weighed 809,000 lb, had 70 in driving
wheels and operated at 240 lb per sq in.

● **RIGHT**
The Baltimore & Ohio Railroad's 4-6-4
Hudson type. Many American railroads used
Hudsons in passenger service. The
superpowered Hudson was the natural
progression from the Pacific type.

READING 4-8-4 NORTHERN TYPE CLASS T1

Date	1945
Builder	Reading Shops, Reading, Pennsylvania, USA
Client	Reading Railroad
Gauge	4 ft 8½ in
Driving wheels	70 in
Capacity	2 cylinders 27 x 32 in
Steam pressure	240 lb
Weight	809,000 lb
Tractive effort	68,000 lb

● **ABOVE**
Milwaukee Road took delivery of Class S-3
Northerns from Alco in 1944. These powerful
locomotives were used for freight and
passenger service but were too heavy to
operate on some routes.

Continued development of the
Hudson type produced some of the finest
passenger locomotives ever built. About
500 Hudson types were built for service
in America.

● **NORTHERNS**
The 4-8-4 Northern type was first
developed in 1927 for the Northern
Pacific. The Northern was an excellent
locomotive for high-speed passenger
service and fast freight service and
remained in production throughout
World War II. Some of the finest
examples of the Northern type were

Union Pacific railroad's 800-class, built
by Alco in 1937; Milwaukee Road's S-
Class, built by Alco in 1944; Santa Fe's
2900 Series, built by Baldwin that same
year; and NYC's 6000 Series
locomotives, built in 1946 and usually
referred to by the railroad as Niagaras
rather than as Northerns.

Some Northerns were delivered in
streamlined shrouds, notably Norfolk &
Western Railroad's J Class and Southern
Pacific's GS-2 to GS-6 Class. (SP's Class
GS-1, GS-7 and GS-8 did not feature
streamlining.)

More than 1,000 Northern types
were built for North American railroads.
Union Pacific has the distinction of
maintaining a Northern well past the
end of steam in the 1950s. In 1996
its famous Northern No. 844 emerged
from a multi-million dollar overhaul
and paraded around the system in
excursion service.

● **RIGHT**
Union Pacific has maintained No. 844. While
used mainly for excursion services, it
occasionally hauls freight. In September 1989,
it led a westbound freight across Nebraska
from Omaha to North Platte.

AMERICAN ELECTRIC
AND EARLY DIESELS

The first use of electric locomotives in
the United States of America was in the
Baltimore Railway Tunnel, by the
Baltimore & Ohio Railroad (B&O)
in 1895.

● ELECTRICS
Electrification gained popularity after the
turn of the century and through the
1930s many American railroads
electrified portions of their main lines.
Most notable were the Pennsylvania
Railroad (PPR) extensive 11,000-volt
alternating current (a.c.) electrification in
New York, New Jersey, Maryland and
Pennsylvania; the New York Central
(NYC) 660-volt direct current (d.c.)
third-rail electrification; New Haven's
11,000-volt a.c. suburban main-line
electrification in Connecticut; and
Milwaukee Road's famous 3,000-volt d.c.
overhead electrification through the
mountains of Montana, Idaho and
Washington State. PRR owned many
classes of electric locomotives, from the

small 0-C-0 switchers, Class B1, to the
famous Raymond Loewy-styled 4-C+C-
4, Class GG1. The GG1 served PRR and
its successors for nearly 50 years.

NYC operated several classes of
motors in the New York City area. Its
first electric, Class S1, No. 6000, was in
service from 1904 until the 1970s.

PENNSYLVANIA RAILROAD CLASS GG1 ELECTRIC LOCOMOTIVE	
Date	1934–43
Builder	Baldwin, General Electric, Juniata Shops
Client	Pennsylvania Railroad
Gauge	4 ft 8½ in
Voltage	11,000 volts a.c.
Power	4,680 hp
Weight	460,000 lb
Tractive effort	75,000 lb

● **BELOW**
The PRR operated 139 GG1 electrics in freight
and passenger service on its electrified lines.
These Raymond Loewy-styled locomotives
operated for nearly 50 years.

New Haven's electrics could operate
from both 660-volt d.c. third rail and
11,000-volt a.c. overhead wire. New
Haven used EF-class motors in freight
service and EP-class motors in passenger
service. Its last passenger electrics were
10 EP-5s, delivered by General Electric
in 1955.

● **ABOVE**
A PRR GG1 leads a high-speed passenger-train
through Frankford Junction, near
Philadelphia, Pennsylvania, in 1959.

● **LEFT**
The Rio Grande Zephyr on the Denver & Rio
Grande Western Railroad, seen at Thistle,
Colorado, in 1982.

● LEFT
One of the New Haven railroad's EP-5 passenger electrics leads a train through Sunnyside Yard, in Queens, New York, in 1960. New Haven's 10 EP-5s, built by General Electric in 1955, were the railroad's last new passenger electrics.

Milwaukee Road's most famous electrics were its 6-D+D-6, Class EP-2, Bipolars, built by GE in 1918 for use on its Washington State lines; and its 1949 GE-built Little Joes for its Montana and Idaho lines. These double-ended, baby-faced locomotives were intended for operation in Russia but not delivered because of the start of the Cold War. Hence their nickname, after Joseph Stalin. Milwaukee discontinued the last of its electric operations in 1974, and six years later abandoned its tracks to the Pacific Coast.

● **DIESEL-ELECTRIC INTRIGUE**

America's first successful commercial diesel-electric was a 60 ton, 300 hp boxcab built by Alco-GE-Ingersol Rand for the Central Railroad of New Jersey in 1925. At first, the diesel-electric was primarily used for switching, but its passenger application became evident with the introduction of the Budd-built Pioneer Zephyr on the Burlington railroad in 1934. This articulated, streamlined, stainless-steel wonder changed the way railroads viewed the diesel-electric.

In 1939, General Motors Electro-Motive Corporation introduced the FT, a 1,350-hp, streamlined locomotive designed to be operated in sets of four in heavyfreight service. This amazing locomotive outperformed contemporary steam locomotives in nearly every service in which it was tested. The diesel had proved it could handle all kinds of service and, in most respects, in a more cost-efficient way than steam. Only World War II prolonged the inevitable. Following the war, the diesel-electric quickly took over from the steam locomotive. By the mid-1950s, many railroads had completely replaced

locomotive fleets with new diesels. By 1960, the steam locomotive was relegated to the status of a historical curiosity.

The diesel-electric enabled American railroads to "electrify" their lines without stringing wires. In some cases, the diesel-electric replaced true electric operations as well.

● BELOW TOP
The Electro-Motive E7 was one of the most popular passenger locomotives. More than 500 were built. Here, a pair of the Louisville & Nashville railroad's E7s rest at Louisville, Kentucky, in 1958.

● BELOW BOTTOM
Electro-Motive Corporation's EAs built in 1937 for the Baltimore & Ohio railroad were the first streamlined passenger diesel-electrics not part of an articulated-train set.

AMERICAN INTERURBANS

Between the 1890s and World War I, lightweight interurban electric railways were built throughout the United States of America. Their greatest concentration was in the Northeast and Midwest.

● INTERURBANS' PERFORMANCE ACROSS AMERICA

Interurbans were mainly passenger carriers, but many developed freight business as well. Interurbans were badly affected when automobile travel became popular, and very few interurban companies survived the Great Depression of the 1930s. A handful of interurban lines operated passenger services into the 1950s and early 1960s. Others survived as freight carriers. Only a few segments of the once-great interurban system exist today, mostly as freight carriers. Three are still electrified, and one line, the Chicago, South Shore & South Bend, still carries passengers.

● INTERURBAN CARS

Early interurban car design emulated that of steam railroad passenger cars. Ornate, heavyweight, wooden cars prevailed until about 1915 when steel cars became standard. Interurban cars were built by several companies including the American Car Company, Brill, Cincinnati Car Company, Holman Car Company and the Jewett Car Company, most of which also built street cars and elevated rapid-transit cars.

● ABOVE

The North Shore operated two articulated, streamlined electric train sets called Electroliners on its high-speed line between Chicago, Illinois, and Milwaukee, Wisconsin. An Electroliner is seen here on the streets of Milwaukee – on 19 July 1958.

● BELOW

The Chicago, South Shore & South Bend Railroad operated a fleet of Standard Steel Car interurban cars. Here, a typical South Shore interurban is seen at Gary, Indiana, in 1958.

The North Shore painted some of its heavyweight interurban cars to make it appear as if they were modern, stainless-steel, streamlined cars.

CHICAGO, SOUTH SHORE & SOUTH BEND INTERURBAN COACH

Date	1929
Builder	Standard Steel Car
Client	South Shore & South Bend Interurban
Gauge	4 ft 8½ in
Voltage	1,500 d.c.
Axles	Four
Weight	133,600 lb
Propulsion	Westinghouse
Seating	48 seats

A few interurbans ordered high-speed, lightweight cars in the 1930s, notably the Fonda, Johnstown & Gloversville railroad in New York State, which acquired five streamlined Bullet cars from Brill in 1932; the Cincinnati & Lake Erie railroad, which acquired 20 high-speed cars from the Cincinnati Car Company in 1932; and the Northern Indiana Railway, which acquired ten lightweight cars from Cummings in 1930.

● ARTICULATED STREAMLINERS
The Chicago, North Shore & Milwaukee (the North Shore) received two streamlined, articulated interurban train sets from the St Louis Car Company in 1941. Named Electroliners, these flashy trains were painted in a unique emerald- and-salmon multistriped scheme. The North Shore was one of few interurbans integrated with a city rapid-transit system. For more than 20 years, the Electroliners zipped between Milwaukee, Wisconsin, and Chicago's "L" Loop. After the North Shore's demise in 1963, the Electroliners were sold to Philadelphia, where they operated for another ten years as Liberty Liners on the Norristown Highspeed Line (the former Philadelphia & Western). The Illinois Terminal also operated St Louis Car streamlined articulated interurbans.

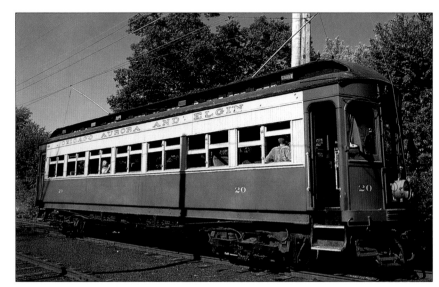

The Chicago, Aurora & Elgin (CA&E) railroad's No. 20 was built by the Niles Car & Manufacturing Company in 1902. It weighs 85,000 lb and seats 52 passengers. The CA&E powered its cars by third-rail and overhead wire.

CANADIAN PASSENGER

In 1948, about 4,100 steam locomotives were serving Canada's two main railroads, Canadian National (CN) and Canadian Pacific (CP).

● LOCOMOTIVE BUILDERS

Two commercial Canadian builders provided most of these locomotives. The Montreal Locomotive Works (MLW), a subsidiary of the American Locomotive Company (Alco), built more than 3,600 steam locomotives between the turn of the century and the early-1950s when it switched to producing diesel-electric locomotives. The Canadian Locomotive Company (CLC), founded in the 1850s, built more than 2,500 steam locomotives, including about 500 export models. In 1950, CLC was given the licence to build Fairbanks-Morse diesel-electric locomotives.

● CANADIAN NATIONAL

The CN railroad introduced the 4-8-4 to Canada in 1927, only a few months after Northern Pacific first tried it in the United States of America. CN called the 4-8-4 the Confederation type and during 20 years ordered more than 200 for freight and passenger service. Of CN's 4-8-4s, 11 were streamlined. One of the most impressive types of 4-8-4 was CN's Class U-2-h, intended for dual service. They operated at 250 lb per sq in,

● ABOVE

Canadian Pacific's most famous locomotives were its Royal Hudsons, built by the Montreal Locomotive Works from 1938. Like many CP steam-locomotives, they were semi-streamlined and had recessed headlights.

● BELOW

Canadian Pacific Railway G-5 4-6-2s, Nos. 1246 and 1293, pictured at Brockways Mills, Vermont, USA.

weighed 400,300 lb, featured 73 in driving wheels, and produced a 56,000 lb tractive effort. CN also maintained a fleet of 4-8-2 Mountain types, many working exclusively in passenger service.

● **CANADIAN PACIFIC**

The late-era steam locomotives of CP feature several distinctive hallmarks. Most were semi-streamlined and featured

centred, recessed headlights. As with CN locomotives, CP used vestibule cabs to give crews greater comfort when operating in extremely cold temperatures.

CP preferred 4-6-2 Pacific types and 4-6-4 Hudson types for its passenger service. It began buying Pacifics in 1906 and continued acquiring them until 1948. Its Hudsons were notable locomotives, with outstanding performance records and excellent aesthetic qualities. Some CP Hudsons regularly operated on 800-mile-long runs. Its best-known 4-6-4s were its H1 Royal Hudsons, so named because two of their class hauled the special trains that brought King George VI and Queen Elizabeth across Canada in 1939. The Royal Hudsons were decorated with an embossed crown.

● ABOVE
A Canadian National 4-8-4, No. 6218, races with a passenger excursion. CN owned more 4-8-4s than any other railroad.

● ABOVE
A Canadian National 4-8-4, No. 6218, rolls a passenger-train off a bridge in 1964.

CANADIAN PACIFIC CLASS H1D, 4-6-4 ROYAL HUDSON	
Date	1938
Builder	Montreal Locomotive Works
Client	Canadian Pacific
Gauge	4 ft 8½ in
Driving wheels	75 in
Capacity	2 cylinders 22 x 30 in
Steam pressure	275 lb
Weight	628,500 lb
Tractive effort	45,300 lb

● LEFT
Canadian National railroad preferred four-coupled steam locomotives and owned many Mikados, Mountains and Confederations (known elsewhere as Northerns). Here, a 4-8-2 Mountain Class N-7b, No. 6017, rests at Turcot Yard, Montreal.

CANADIAN FREIGHT

Canadian National was a publicly owned company formed in 1922 from a number of failing railroad lines. It was the larger line of the two Canadian systems and spanned Canada from coast to coast.

● CANADIAN NATIONAL

In the 1920s, the unified CN acquired many 4-8-2 Mountain types and smaller 2-8-2 Mikados. In 1927 it was one of the first railroads to adopt the 4-8-4 Northern type, which it called the Confederation type. CN and its American subsidiary, Grand Trunk Western (GTW), eventually owned more than 200 4-8-4s, far more than any other North American railroad. These high horsepower 4-8-4s were ideal suited for heavy freight service and passenger service.

In 1929, CN experimented with an alternative form of motive power. It ordered two diesel-electrics from Westinghouse and was the first North American railroad to use the diesel in main-line service. However, these experimental locomotives were unsuccessful and not duplicated.

● **LEFT**
While CN preferred four-coupled steam locomotives such as 4-8-2 Mountains, CP embraced three-coupled locomotives. CP had many 4-6-2 Pacifics and used them in all sorts of service. Here, a CP 4-6-2 leads a mixed train at Jackman, Maine, USA, in 1958.

● **LEFT**
A 40-ton Shay "Old One Spot", standard gauge, built in 1910: the last of the woodburners.

Ultimately, CN converted from steam to diesel operations, but at a more gradual rate than railroads in the USA.

● CANADIAN PACIFIC

Privately owned CP took a different approach to its freight locomotives

from CN. Where CN used many four-coupled locomotives, 4-8-2s, 4-8-4s, etc., CP preferred three-coupled locomotives for many applications. It owned many 4-6-2 Pacific types and 4-6-4 Hudson types. It used light Pacifics in branch-line freight service as

● **RIGHT**
A Canadian National 4-8-4, No. 6168, leads a mixed train near Brantford, Ontario, in 1959. CN used many 4-8-4s in freight and passenger service.

CANADIAN PACIFIC CLASS T1b, 2-10-4 SELKIRK TYPE

Date	1929–49
Builder	Montreal Locomotive Works
Client	Canadian Pacific
Gauge	4 ft 8½ in
Driving wheels	63 in
Capacity	2 cylinders 25 x 32 in
Steam pressure	285 lb
Weight	447,000 lb (engine only)
Tractive effort	76,905 lb

well as in passenger service. CP was also one of the few railroads to employ its Hudsons in freight service. Most railroads used this type exclusively for passenger trains.

CP did own some big locomotives. In 1928 it built two 4-8-4s but acquired no more. However, for heavy freight service in the Canadian Rockies, it owned 36 semi-streamlined 2-10-4 Texas-types that it called Selkirks. These locomotives were well suited for steep grades and heavy tonnage and performed well. In 1931, CP built an experimental three-cylinder 2-10-4. This locomotive was not particularly successful, CP did not bother to duplicate it and it was eventually scrapped.

● **ABOVE**
A Canadian National 2-8-0 Consolidation sits at Turcot Yard, Montreal. Most CN steam locomotives were built by Montreal Locomotive Works.

● **ABOVE**
A 45-ton, two-truck Climax logging locomotive, No. 9, built in 1912.

● **LEFT**
In the 1920s, the newly formed Canadian National began buying many 2-8-2 Mikados.

THE PRUSSIAN INFLUENCE

Prussian influence is seen by many to be confined to the large class of 4-6-0 locomotives known as the P8. After Germany's unification in 1871 as an imperial power, Prussia continued to go its own way in railway matters. Other states in the German Empire followed suit under Prussia's sway.

● THE EARLY DAYS

At the end of the 19th century, most railway locomotive authorities were trying to cope with the pace of advance in design, Prussia included. Because of the fairly level nature of Prussian territory, lightweight locomotives with a fair turn of speed lasted for many years and in various guises. Compounding was in fashion and classes were turned out seemingly almost at random, some being compound locomotives and others simple locomotives.

● ABOVE
The Prussian P8 also lasted to the end of the days of steam in West Germany. Here, in the late 1960s, No. 038 509-6 trundles under a bridge.

PRUSSIAN P8	
Date	1906
Builder	Schwarzkopff, Berlin
Client	Prussian State Railways
Gauge	1,435 mm
Class	Prussian P8; Deutsche Reichsbahn (DR) 38
Type	4-6-0
Driving wheels	1,750 mm
Capacity	2 cylinders 575 x 630 mm
Weight in working order	78.2 tonnes
Maximum service speed	100 kph

● THE SCHMIDT SUPERHEATER

Then came a most important event for Prussia and railway administrations worldwide. This was the development of a successful superheater. Steam was dried in a further set of tubes in the boiler to remove water drops in suspension. This superheated steam worked far more efficiently than those preceding it.

In the early 1890s, a Prussian physicist working in this field, Dr Wilhelm Schmidt, was encouraged to try out his results on the Prussian State Railways (PSR) system, by Mr Geheimiath Garbe of PSR. The first Schmidt superheater was fitted in 1897, but, as with many innovations, there were problems of lubrication and leaks. Further, locomotives fitted with superheaters cost more to build. In 1900, a simple 4-4-0 was fitted with the Schmidt superheater and achieved much interest and some success. Compared with nonsuperheated compound 4-4-0s of the same class, the nonsuperheated machines used 12 per cent more coal and 30 per cent more water.

● THE PRUSSIAN P8

The cost-savings of a simple machine against a compound being most

● **RIGHT AND OPPOSITE BOTTOM** Turkish State Railways (TCCD) operates a system separated from the main network to take coal from collieries in the Armutçuk Mountains to the docks at Eregli on the Black Sea. On shed at the port, these Prussian G8-2, two-cylinder 2-8-0s, dating from 1919, are ready for the night's work.

attractive, superheaters began to be fitted more widely and to more types of locomotive, including a class of sturdy 2-6-0 mixed-traffic locomotive. Compounding was not abandoned, however, for high-speed work. PSR had gained experience of the De Glehn compounds and developed their own compound 4-6-0 version. When a simple two-cylinder version for mixed traffic came out in 1906, the scene was set for the expansion of the Prussian Class P8. The first was built by Schwarzkopff of Berlin. Between 1906–21, the PSR bought 3,370 machines. Many others were constructed, including for export. More than 6,000 were built in total. After World War I, reparations demanded from Germany led to the arrival of the P8 in many other countries including Belgium and France.

● **THE WIDER IMPLICATIONS**
Several other classes of Prussian-designed locomotive were also distributed widely, including to Germany's allies, especially Turkey. This distribution and the reparations possibly extended Prussian influence far wider, and interest in these relatively

simple and robust designs grew. The German locomotive-building industry's need to gear up to replace stocks distributed elsewhere increased its design and production capacity. From this, German builders outside Prussia also benefited while, in Germany, the foundations were laid for German State Railways – the Deutsche Reichsbahn (DR) and, after 1945, the Deutsche Bundesbahn (DB).

● **BELOW LEFT**
The Deutsche Bundesbahn (DB) Class 078 4-6-4T lasted right to the end of the days of steam, in the early-1970s in then-West Germany. One of the class is pictured in a familiar role on a light passenger-train. This class, as Prussian Class T18, was built in batches between 1912-27.

● **BELOW**
Also on shed at Eregli in Turkey, in the 1970s, a driver is oiling round on a Prussian Type-G8 44071, an 0-8-0 dating from 1902, before moving off to pick up his train.

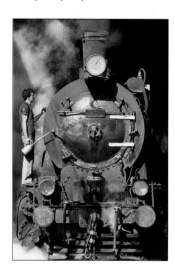

THE REICHSBAHN STANDARDS

After World War I, Germany's need to reorganize its railways led in 1920 to formation of a national system, the Reichsbahn. It is not surprising that Prussian management and methods were prominent.

● **THE FOUNDATIONS**

An engineering-management centre was set up in Berlin. One of its decisions was to produce a series of locomotive classes that would operate across the network. A man called Wagner was placed in charge. In the years to 1939, at least, Wagner's stature as an engineer and manager grew.

● **FIRST STEPS**

One of his first decisions was to categorize all the locomotives from

● **RIGHT**
This unmodified 01-798 had a trailing load of 450 tonnes as it neared Grossenhain, in the then-East Germany, on the 06.37 hours express from Berlin to Dresden in 1977.

various sources under his control. This was so successful that its basic tenets were widely followed elsewhere in the operation. It pointed to strengths and weaknesses in the stock. Once more, Prussian influence emerged.

This is not to say that the other German States' railways had little to offer. Saxony and Württemberg were well advanced. Further, private locomotive builders contributed high technical input to many designs.

KRIEGSLOK – DEUTSCHE REICHSBAHN (DR) CLASS 52

Date	1942
Builder	Borsig of Berlin
Client	Deutsche Reichsbahn
Gauge	1,435 mm
Class	52
Type	2-10-0
Driving wheels	1,400 mm
Capacity	2 cylinders 500 x 600 mm (stroke)
Weight in working order	85.3 tonnes
Maximum service speed	80 kph

● **RIGHT**
A Class 050 2-10-0, No. 050 383-9, pulling away from Freudenstadt Station in the Black Forest, in the then West Germany of the late 1960s.

● **DESIGN CRITERIA**
Compounding was on the way out. Two-cylinder, simple expansion locomotives were to be adopted, although, in the 1930s, three small specialist classes had three cylinders. Robust engineering was assisted by raising the axleload on main lines to 20.4 tonnes. Ease of maintenance was improved by mounting ancillaries on the boiler and adopting bar-frames as favoured by the locomotive-builders, J.A. Maffei of Munich. Commodious cabs eased the lot of footplate crews. Many other decisions affected components and fittings, some of which carried on Prussian practice. Despite radical changes to external appearance, the Prussian style continued to dominate.

● **STANDARDS AT HOME AND ABROAD**
No fewer than 29 classes were brought into service between 1925–45. They ranged from small classes of 0-6-0T and 2-4-2T, to the 6,292 Class 52 Kriegslok introduced in 1942. These ranged far and wide across Europe, surviving well beyond designers' expectations.

Standard designs proved attractive to other countries. Some bought almost identical designs from German builders, or built them under licence in their own works. For example, Poland had modified Prussian P8s in 1922; Turkey had a range of types in regular use in the 1970s and, in small numbers, even later than this.

Many examples remained in regular use in the former East Germany until the late 1980s. A substantial number, especially of Kriegsloks, have been recovered for restoration and use on special trains in European countries.

● **OPPOSITE**
A Kriegslok of Turkish State Railways (TCDD), No. 56533, pictured about to move off to pick up a freight train in the nearby yard.

● **RIGHT**
Class 01 Pacific 4-6-2s were still working between Berlin and Dresden, Saxony, in the then East Germany, in 1977, when this rural scene was briefly disturbed near Weinböhla.

GÖLSDORF AND THE AUSTRIAN EMPIRE

The Austro-Hungarian Empire, before its
eventual collapse in 1918 as a result of
World War I, was one of the most
powerful political and economic entities
in continental Europe.

● **BACKGROUND**

Its railways' main axis ran generally east-
west with few topographical problems in
the easterly direction from Vienna, in
Austria, to Budapest, in Hungary. To the
south, the only real geographical
challenge between Vienna and Graz, in
Austria, was surmounted by the opening
in 1853 of the Trieste Railway line over
the Austrian Alps and through the 980 m
(3,215 ft) high Semmering Pass. A
similar problem faced railway builders for
the line going southward to Italy from
Innsbruck in Austria. This crossed the
mountains through the 1,369 m (4,494 ft)
high Brenner Pass whose railroad was

completed 1867. Apart from the
relatively level lines to the German
border to the west, other lines westward
tended to be regarded as secondary.
Moreover, they faced the main European
Alpine barrier. The best route was a
single line through Austria's Tirol and
Vorarlberg. This reached Buchs, Kanton
St Gallen on the Swiss border, with hard
climbing on both sides of the 1,798 m
(5,900 ft) high Arlberg Tunnel, 6 km
(3¾ miles) long and opened in 1884.

● **DR KARL GÖLSDORF**

Karl Gölsdorf was born into a railway
family in 1861. By the age of 30 he was
chief mechanical engineer (CME) of the
Austrian State Railway. In the early
1900s, he was made responsible for all
mechanical engineering under the
purview of the Austrian Railway Ministry,
which also influenced the notionally

independent Hungarian railways. His
achievements include the rack-and-pinion
Erzberg line. The 1,533 m (5,032 ft)
high Erzberg Mountain, rich in iron ore,
stands above the mining commune of
Eisenerz in Austria's Styria province.

● **DESIGN PROBLEMS AND
SOLUTIONS**

The empire's level routes required
locomotives capable of sustained high
speed, while the curving, mountainous
lines called for machines capable of a
long, hard slog. Both criteria needed free
steaming. However, Gölsdorf faced the
severe limitation of lightweight track and,
consequently, a maximum axleload of no
more than 14.5 tons.

He achieved high power:weight ratios
by relatively high boiler pressures and by
applying his own dictum that it is easier
to save weight on each of a thousand

● **LEFT**
This scene in
Strasshof
locomotive depot
north of Vienna in
1987 includes BBÖ,
Bundesbahnen
Österreich, class
30.33. This engine
dates from 1895 and
is sporting two
steam domes and
joining-pipe.

● **ABOVE LEFT AND RIGHT**
These locomotives are Gölsdorf designs or derivatives active as late as the 1970s in what was then Yugoslavia.

● **BELOW RIGHT**
The elegance of Gölsdorf's express passenger locomotives is well known. Less well known is this class of three rack-and-pinion locomotives. Its life was spent mostly on trains loaded with iron ore from the Erzberg, the Iron Mountain at Eisenerz, in Austria's Styria province, to the point where trains were handed over to pure adhesion traction at Vordernberg.

GÖLSDORF'S DESIGN FOR THE RACK AND PINION ERZBERG LINE

Date	1912
Builder	Dr Karl Gölsdorf
Gauge	1,435 mm
Class	BBO 269; OBB 197
Type	BBO category F: Whyte notation 0-12-0T
Capacity adhesion:	2 cylinders 570 x 520 mm
pinion:	2 cylinders 520 x 450 mm
Coupled wheel diameter	1,030 mm
Weight in working order	88 tonnes
Maximum service speed	Adhesion, 30 kph; rack, 15 kph

small parts than on a few large ones. Wide firegrates helped to ensure a plentiful supply of steam. Very large driving wheels on express locomotives, up to 7 ft in diameter, gave the opportunity for high speed. Up to 12 small coupled wheels offered the adhesion and formed part of the tractive-effort calculations for heavy hauling in the mountains.

● **COMPOUNDING**
Gölsdorf's designs are often regarded as unusual. One obvious feature was visible early on. Two domes were mounted on the boiler barrel, both to collect steam. They were linked by a large pipe through which steam from one passed to the regulator in the other. More important

was a hidden device. Gölsdorf was a great proponent of compounding, often using just two cylinders, one high- and the other low-pressure. Difficulty was often experienced in starting compounds from rest. Instead of the usual starting-valve requiring skilled operation, high-pressure steam was automatically admitted to the low-pressure cylinder when the valve gear was fully in fore or back gear.

His designs were generally adopted by the Hungarian railways, although in some cases they used simple machines based on Gölsdorf's compounds. After the empire's break-up, many of his numerous types of locomotive could be found in Czecho-slovakia, Hungary and Yugoslavia where, as in Austria, some can be seen today.

THE FRENCH
INFLUENCE – STEAM

1900 to 1950 truly was the "Golden Age" for steam in France. Designers were pushing at the frontiers of knowledge of locomotive design and performance. The age also bred a class of driver who not only had to learn about the new technology but also had to adapt driving techniques to take best advantage of it. The French *mécanicien* was an outstanding footplate technician.

● **RIGHT**
French railways had a wide range of tank locomotives for local passenger and freight work. These Class 141TAs are former Paris-Orleans railway machines built between 1911–23.

● **COMPOUNDING**
To a railway historian, compounding is immediately identified with France and two names: Alfred De Glehn and André Chapelon. De Glehn was born in Britain.

Compounding works like this. A basic steam locomotive creates steam under pressure in its boiler. The steam expands in cylinders to drive the pistons and is then exhausted to the atmosphere. But a lot of power is still left in the exhausting steam. If this steam is channelled to a larger, low-pressure cylinder, this power, otherwise wasted, can be used to save fuel and water.

As with much engineering, there are disadvantages. The machines are more complicated. They demand top-quality maintenance and skilled driving.

● **DESIGNERS AND THEIR WORK**
Other French engineers who made great contributions to worldwide development included Gaston Du Bousquet, a contemporary of De Glehn, and, towards the end of the steam era, Mark de Caso. Chapelon always acknowledged Du Bousquet's groundwork, which led to some of his successes.

As always, locomotive designers had to work under constraints. In France, where

railways have been strictly controlled since 1857, there was a requirement before World War II for the shortest possible journey-times to be achieved without exceeding 75 mph. This meant that uphill speeds with heavy loads had to be high. The De Glehn compounds built up to 1914, economical and free running, were more than adequate in their day. As loads increased and they had to be worked harder, however, efficiency fell away, and little real work was obtained from a four-cylinder compound's low-pressure cylinders.

● **LEFT**
Much painstaking work was required to restore this classic "Mountain", No. 241A 65, to working order. It was built by Fives-Lille (Works No. 4714/1931) and is shown on shed at St Sulpice, Neuchâtel, Switzerland, in 1994.

● **ABOVE LEFT**
This former Paris-Orleans railway's 231E
Pacific heads the Flêche d'Or Calais-Paris
express in the later days of steam, as shown by
the standard rolling stock. In its heyday, it was
a luxury train, but the locomotive, a Du
Bousquet/Chapelon design for the Paris-
Orleans railway, is truly from the golden age.

● **ABOVE RIGHT**
These 2-8-2 tanks simmering on shed recall
scenes once familiar in a typical French
roundhouse.

SNCF (ETAT) 241A

Date	1927
Builder	Compagnie de Fives-Lille, Fives, France
Client	Société Nationale des Chemins de Fer (SNCF)
Gauge	1,435 mm
Type	241 (Whyte notation, 4-8-2)
Driving wheels	1,790 mm
Capacity	2 cylinders 510 x 650 mm 2 cylinders 720 x 700 mm
Weight in working order	114.6 tonnes
Maximum service speed	120 kph

● **REDOUBLING POWER AND
EFFICIENCY**
In the late 1920s, Chapelon began to
stand out as a great railway engineer. He
had entered railway service in 1919 but
in 1924 joined a telephone company. His
research abilities, recognized while he
was a student, then led to him accepting
an appointment in the Paris-Orleans
railway's research department. There,
Monsieur Paul Billet charged him to
improve specific machines' exhaust
systems. This was the platform on which
his career really began.

Studies had confirmed that power was
being wasted in getting steam from boiler
to cylinder. The reasons included

inadequate and indirect steam passages.
Redesign under Chapelon's expert
guidance led almost to redoubling the
power and efficiency of rebuilt
compound locomotives.

However, these improvements
applied equally to simple expansion
locomotives, and the techniques were
eagerly adopted across the world. They
strengthened the argument of those who
considered that simple locomotives with
high superheat were, overall, more
economical. To Chapelon's credit, he was
not a slavish devotee of compounding,
and he caused similar significant
improvements to classes of simple
expansion locomotives.

● **LEFT**
231 G 558 drifts into
the port of Le
Havre, northern
France, with a train
of 1930s stock. Were
it not for the
overhead-line
equipment, the
scene might have
been soon after
1935 when the SNCF
rebuilt this 1922-
constructed
Batignolles Pacific.
In fact, the picture
was taken in 1992.

THE SWISS INFLUENCE – MOUNTAIN RAILWAYS

Mountain railways are usually powered either on the funicular principle (the weight of a descending car pulls another up) or on the "rack-and-pinion" principle of toothed rails.

● THE RIGGENBACH SYSTEM

The first successful rack-and-pinion system was developed not in Switzerland but in the USA. Development was proceeding in both countries, but neither of their two respective engineers knew of the other's work.

In Switzerland, Niklaus Riggenbach took out a patent on 12 August 1863 but did not develop it then. In 1869, he heard about the railway up 800 m (2,624 ft) high Mount Washington, in Berkshire County, USA, with its rack system designed by Sylvester Marsh. He visited that railway and on his return successfully developed his "ladder rack". Its first application was to a short quarry line at Ostermundigen, near Bern, in 1870. The locomotive that worked the

RIGI BAHN NO. 7

Date	1873
Builder	Swiss Locomotive and Machine Works (SLM), Winterthur
Client	Rigi Bahn
Gauge	1,435 mm
Rack system	Riggenbach
Capacity	2 cylinders 270 x 400 mm
Weight in working order	15.1 tonnes (as built)
Maximum speed	7.5 kph

● BELOW
The first SLM-built steam railway locomotive, Rigi Bahn No. 7, was taken from Luzern Transport Museum in 1995 and restored by SLM for the 125th anniversary of Switzerland's Vitznau-Rigi Bahn (VRB) in 1996, when it was pictured pushing a fully loaded vintage coach from Rigi Staffel to Rigi Kulm summit station.

line, "Gnom", has been preserved.

The success was soon followed by another when his system was applied to the Vitznau-Rigi Bahn (VRB), a standard-gauge line linking Vitznau, on Lake Lucerne, with the isolated 1,800 m (5,906 ft) high Rigi Mountain. This line

● **RIGHT**
There is no difficulty in fitting pinion gear to
electric vehicles. The 800 mm-gauge Wengernalp
Bahn (WAB), which provides the intermediate
stage of the journey from Interlaken to the
4,758 m (13,642 ft)-high Jungfrau Mountain in
central Switzerland's Bernese Alps, uses the
Riggenbach-Pauli rack to reach Kleine
Scheidegg. These trains are pictured at
Grindelwald Grund in 1989 before tackling their
climb. Some stock dates from 1947.

● **BELOW**
The Locher rack's unique construction is shown
in this picture, taken in 1991 from the traverser
well at the Pilatus railway depot, Alpnachstad,
at the foot of Mount Pilatus, near Luzern.

● **LEFT**
The opening of the
Filisur-Bever section
of Switzerland's
Rhaetische Bahn in
1903 signalled the
conquest of river,
valley and mountain
to reach a plateau at
1,800 m (6,000 ft).
Steam was the
original power but
in 1921 the 61-tonne
electric locomotives
pictured here came
on the scene.

or system celebrated its centenary in
1996 by operating one of the original
vertical-boilered locomotives, No. 7, the
first locomotive to be built by the Swiss
Locomotive and Machine Works (SLM),
of Winterthur, near Zürich.

● **THE RIGGENBACH-LOCHER
SYSTEM**
It was Riggenbach who came up with
the germ of an idea from the fitting of
hooks that ran under the rails on the
funicular from Territet to Glion near
Montreux at the eastern end of Lake
Geneva. The actual design is credited to
Colonel Eduard Locher who became
engineer to the Pilatus line in
Unterwalden Canton, central
Switzerland, with its 1:2 gradients.
The design amounted to a pair of
horizontally mounted guide pinion
wheels with deep, plain flanges which
run underneath the specially designed
rack-rail. In effect, traction and guidance

were performed by the rack-rail
and pinion wheels. The rails on which
the carriage wheels run are merely
for balance.

● **ADHESION LINES**
Numerous, mostly metre-gauge, lines
wind their way into the mountains, in
some cases tackling gradients of about
1:13 (7.7 per cent) without rack
assistance. Two examples are popular
with tourists. One is the Montreux-
Oberland-Bernoise, which runs from
Montreux through valley and alp to
Zweisimmen. The other is the extensive
spread of metre-gauge routes on the
Rhaetische Bahn, which covers the
Rhaetian Alps and Switzerland's largest
canton, Graubünden (Grisons).
    The Rhaetische Bahn offers specta-
cular scenery and benefits from remarkable engineering feats, which enable the
line to reach the fertile flatlands of the
Engadine, that is the 97 km (60 mile)

long valley of the River Inn, some 1,800
m (6,000 ft) above sea level. Much of the
area is devoted to sports in winter when
there is only one reliable means of access
and egress – the railway. Spirals and
tunnelling had to be used similar to that
adopted by Swiss Federal Railways on two
earlier lines. The section of the SFR over
the St Gotthard Pass, with an inter-
cantonal 15 km (9½ mile) long tunnel at
1,154 m (3,788 ft), completed in
1872–81, links Göschenen and Airolo
and the Bern-Loetschberg-Simplon line
between Frütigen and Brig with the
Loetschberg Tunnel.
    The 20 km (12½ mile) long Simplon
Tunnel built in 1898–1905, between Brig
and Domodossola, lies partly in
Switzerland and partly in Italy. In its day
it was the world's longest railway tunnel,
famous for carrying the Simplon–Orient
Express, with connections, from Calais,
over the Alps at 705 m (2,313 ft), to
Istanbul, Athens and Asia Minor.

SOUTHERN EUROPE – IBERIAN, ITALIAN AND GREEK PENINSULAS

The railways of Peninsular Europe – Iberia (Spain and Portugal), Italy and Greece – have long been concerned not only with national and international services but with intercontinental links between Europe and Africa, across the Western and Eastern Mediterranean Sea. Since 1869, proposals to build a rail-and-road fixed link between Spain and Morocco, across the Strait of Gibraltar, making Tangier the gateway to Africa, have been discussed. (Similarly, proposals to link Eurasia and North America by a rail tunnel across the Bering Strait, between Russia's Siberia and Alaska, have been discussed since 1905.)

● **SPAIN**

In Spain, locomotive design and construction was well developed and most steam locomotives not only entered the 20th century but continued to operate beyond the 1950s – apart from those most heavily used or taxed by mountainous terrain. Nevertheless, from the 1920s, many large and well-proportioned loco-motives were obtained for the standard gauge from various domestic and foreign builders, the 4-8-2 wheel arrangement

● **LEFT**
A large Mallet-type metre-gauge 2-4-6-0T, pictured at Chaves, northern Portugal, in 1974.

● **LEFT**
In Greece, the sun glints on a chunky USA-built 2-8-0 of a general type familiar across Europe immediately after World War II.

● **BELOW**
Locomotives 2-8-2 No. 7108 and doubled-domed Es Class No. 7721 head a special train at Diakofto, Greece in 1980.

being preferred. There were even Garratts, built in 1930 for passenger work.

Electrification began in 1911 on 21 km (13 miles) of steeply graded line on the Spanish Southern Railway between Gérgal and Santa Fé de Montdújar, in the Sierra Nevada of Almeria province, and was slowly extended to Almeria town, on the coast, 44 km (27 miles) in all. Overhead-line a.c. 5.5kv 3 phase was used. Some massive locomotives were supplied for these lines, including 12 2CC2s in 1928 from Babcock & Wilcox-Brown Boveri.

Steady progress came to a grinding halt with the Civil War (1936–9), but new steam and electrics began operating fairly quickly thereafter. Further, the process of building new lines to make a more effective network continued, forming a firm base for the sound rail system Spain has today.

● FAR RIGHT
Visible on FS Italia
2-8-0 No. 741 046
are the Crosti
preheater drum,
beneath the
smokebox door, and
the exhaust
replacing the
conventional
chimney.

F S ITALIA CLASS 741

Date	1911 (rebuilt 1955)
Builder	Breda
Client	F.S. Italia (rebuild)
Gauge	1,435 mm
Class	741 (rebuilt from 740)
Driving wheels	140 (Whyte notation 2-8-0)
Capacity	2 cylinders 540 x 700 mm
Driving wheel diameter	1,370 mm
Weight in working order	68.3 tonnes
Maximum service speed	65 kph

● BELOW
This Alco 1,500 hp
diesel-electric,
delivered in 1948, is
one of 12 in the van
of Portugal's diesel
revolution. It is
pictured at Tunes,
Algarve, in 1996.

● PORTUGAL

At the turn of the century, Portugal's steam-locomotive stock was varied and of good lineage. It included De Glehn compounds built in 1898-1903 and typical Henschel outline 4-6-0s, built at Kossel, Germany. Indeed, most European builders of note were represented. It was 1924 before Pacifics arrived from Henschel. Several series of 2-8-0s for freight came into service between 1912-24, built by Schwarzkopf of Berlin and North British of the United Kingdom. The first 4-8-0 arrived from Henschel in 1930. Tank locomotives ranging from 0-4-0T to 2-8-4T helped to cover remaining duties, including suburban passenger-train services.

The metre gauge had some fine machines, many of them big Mallet 2-4-6-0T tanks. The suburban services around Oporto, the country's second-largest city, were shared by 0-4-4-0Ts and 2-8-2Ts dating from 1931.

● ITALY

Italy's steam development was reasonably conventional for the period, subject to disruption in World Wars I and II. The unusual took the form of a novel and effective preheating system for feed water. Dr Ing Piero Crosti designed boilers in which combustion gases pass in the normal way through the main, simple boiler and then in reverse direction through a drum or drums. The feed water introduced into the drum(s) thereby captured more heat from flue gases and reduced scale on the firebox wall. This cut fuel costs but the locomotives' conventional appearance suffered. They had no obvious chimney and exhaust gases were disposed of by a series of pipes near the boiler's rear.

Italy is probably best known in the diesel world for its export of railcars. The names Fiat and Breda are on workplates across the world. These companies began to develop in this field in the mid-1930s, as did Ganz of Hungary. The Fiat railcar started a vogue in 1935 for wheel spats over the bogie wheels, as in aircraft of the day. FS Italia Class Aln 56 was just one example.

● GREECE

In Greece, locomotives were haphazardly obtained from various builders and by purchase of secondhand engines from Germany, Austria and Italy. USA-built locomotives were brought to Greece in 1914 and, again, after damage done to the railways in World War II.

SCANDINAVIAN RAILWAYS

From 1900 the railways of the Scandinavian countries – Norway and Sweden forming the Scandinavian Peninsula and Denmark and Finland respectively to its south and east – were gradually extended, in some cases upgrading from metre to standard gauge, especially in Norway, and moved from steam to electrification, except for Finland whose 805-unit fleet included 766 steam locomotives (95 per cent) as late as 1958.

Apart from Denmark, whose insular component presented other physical difficulties, problems facing the railways were the same as in all cold countries. Frost heave disturbed the permanent way in the level wet areas. Heavy snow, with the ever-present risk of avalanche, was a burden in the mountains of Norway and northern Sweden.

● DENMARK

Denmark remains different from the other Scandinavian countries because of its islands, its population density and its closely sited communities. Here, speed and frequency of services became paramount together with the desire,

● **RIGHT AND OPPOSITE BOTTOM LEFT AND RIGHT** These pictures of steam in Finland capture the sense of an age long past and illustrate Russian design influence. The balloon stack and high stacking-rails on the tender of the wood-burner, No. 1163, can be seen.

● **BELOW RIGHT** The simple outlines of this 1-C-1 diesel, No. HP 15, of the Danish Hjörringer Privatbanen, the railway operating in north-east Jutland's Hjörring county, are appropriate for this workhorse. It was built in about 1935 by Frichs and is pictured at Randers, the east Jutland seaport.

gradually being achieved, to link the mainland Jutland Peninsula to all the islands and to the Scandinavian Peninsula at Malmo by bridge and tunnel rather than conveying trains on albeit very efficient train ferries.

In the 1930s, route length was 5,233 km (3,250 miles), of which only 2,512 km (1,560 miles), that is 48 per cent, was state-owned. The level terrain put no great demands on steam locomotives and it was the light diesel-

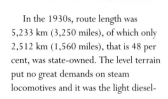

● **LEFT** This 2-6-0T No. 7 sports typical features of Danish steam locomotives, including the smokebox saddle and the national colours in the band around the chimney. Vintage coaches with clerestorey roofs and torpedo vents enhance the nostalgic scene at Helsingor, near Copenhagen, on the Danish island of Zeeland, in 1980.

● LEFT
One of the later versions of the Lyntog ("Lightning") train pictured at Struen, western Jutland, Denmark, in 1980. The four-car unit is powered by a Maybach diesel engine with Voith (Heidenheim, Germany) hydraulic transmission. The power-car is Class MA, No. 467.

railcar that became attractive for passenger work as an alternative to steam.

Electrification came late to Denmark, starting with the suburban system in the capital, Copenhagen, in 1934 employing a line voltage of 1,500 dc. The state system owned a good stock of steam power, mostly built in Germany, but, to develop high-speed services, three-car diesel-electric units called Lyntog ("Lightning") were introduced, which cut journey times dramatically.

● FINLAND

From 1809 to 1917, Finland was part of what was then the Russian Empire and so adopted the Russian 5 ft gauge for main lines and 2 ft 5½ in gauge for minor lines. The terrain was relatively level and, in the earlier part of the 20th century, schedules were not demanding, so that comparatively light, often woodburning, locomotives were sufficient. In the latter days of steam, a small class of coalfired Pacifics with good lines and particularly commodious cabs worked the heaviest passenger services. Local and semifast services around Helsinki, the capital, were served by the neat, most attractive Class N1, built by Hanomag in Germany.

● SWEDEN

The "Golden Age" of Sweden's railways may be said to be firmly linked to the enormous supplies of iron ore in the inhospitable mountains on the northern borders of Sweden and Norway. Near the town of Kiruna, at 509 m (1,670 ft) above sea level Sweden's highest, established mines work night and day. Some 16 million tons were produced in 1960, the bulk being moved by rail for export.

Electrification of the lines at 16,000 volt single phase ac 16⅔ Hz began in 1910

with the Frontier Railway between Lulea and Rikseransen. By 1914, the first of the massive electric locomotives 1+CC+1 for freight and B-B+B-B were being delivered by the builders ASEA/Siemens. Electrification continued apace until, by 1923, some 450 km (280 miles) had been completed. Even more powerful locomotives were provided, ten -D- for freight, producing 1,200 hp and capable of working in multiple, as well as two 2,400 hp B-B+B-B passenger machines.

For general electrification, SJ, the Swedish State Railway, decided on a single class of locomotive to work passenger and freight trains. 1-C-1,

whose gearing can easily be changed to operate either 500-ton passenger-trains at 65 mph or 900-ton freight trains at 45 mph. Electrification did not supplant steam rapidly. Main routes were electrified in the 1930s with considerable success, including the Stockholm–Gothenburg line.

In the early days, locomotives were bought from Britain. Later, designers adapted and developed them to suit local needs. This may be why inside-cylinders continued to be used long after most mainland countries had adopted the more convenient outside form. The practice continued until in 1930 the

Swedish Motala works built a massive inside-cylinder 4-6-0 for the private Kalmar Railways operating in the south-eastern province of Kalmar.

The private Traffic-Ab Grangesberg–Oxelosunds Jarnvagar (TGO), basically an iron-ore mining company, had three noncondensing turbine locomotives in its stock, which achieved a degree of successful operation.

The three-cylinder locomotive was rare in Sweden. In 1927, Nydkvist and Holm of Trollhättan, Sweden, built a class for the Bergslagernas Railway. This class's golden days on the expresses between Gothenburg and Mellerud, on Lake Vanern, ended with electrification in 1939.

As late as 1955, 10 per cent of train miles were operated by steam and 63

per cent by electricity. The remaining 27 per cent was diesel, but during the period under consideration, up to 1950, diesel traction had yet to become significant.

● NORWAY

Norway, politically linked with Sweden under the Swedish Crown between 1814–1905, is the most mountainous of Scandinavian countries. Its railway lines spread out from the capital, Oslo, like fingers, seeking natural routes to a scattered population.

Norway's railways developed late and in a scattered fashion. In the more benign terrain north of Oslo, steam traction was successful. British designs were the basis for further development.

Locomotives had been bought from the USA since 1879. When purchase of new locomotives became necessary during World War I, Baldwin Works of Philadelphia, USA, were asked to supply 2-8-0s, ostensibly to Norwegian design. Certainly, the boiler fittings and enclosed cab were Norwegian, but the rest was

SWEDISH STATE RAILWAY (SJ) 4-6-0	
Date	1918
Builder	Nyakvist and Holm, Trollhättan, Sweden
Client	Swedish State Railway (SJ)
Gauge	1,435 mm
Class	B
Driving wheels	1,750 mm
Capacity	2 cylinders 590 x 620 mm
Weight in working order	69.2 tonnes (excluding tender)
Maximum service speed	90 kph

pure Baldwin. Two 0-10-0 yard-shunters
came from the same source in 1916, as
well as three 2-8-2 for freight. In 1919, a
2-6-2T arrived, which now had the
stamp of real Norwegian design.

Later classes show German influence.
An unusual design of 1935 was a 2-8-4, a
wheel arrangement previously seen only
in Austria for an express-locomotive. The
class were four-cylinder compounds for
the Dovre line, across the Dovrefjell, the
2,285 m (7,565 ft) high central
Norwegian plateau, between Dombås
and Trondheim (formerly Trondhjem),
the seaport and the country's third
largest city. The first engine was called
The Dovre Giant. However, much
smaller and ageing 2-6-0s and 4-6-0s
worked main-line and branch services
into the mid-1960s.

Electrification, especially in the far
north, followed the Swedish pattern.
Because there was plenty of water for
hydroelectric power, electrification began
in 1922 between Oslo and Drammen,
the seaport on a branch of Oslo Fjord.

At the same time, work was in hand to
link the main centres to Oslo. Trondheim
was first in 1921, followed by Christiansand,
the seaport on the Skagerrak in 1938 and
Stavanger seaport in 1944.

Almost all the route mileage of about
4,300 km (2,700 miles) is state-owned,
about a third of which is electrified at
15 kv single phase 16⅔ Hz. Few narrow-

gauge systems operated by state and
private companies have survived.

Narvik, which exports iron ore, is the
terminus for the railway that cuts across
the peninsula from the Swedish port of
Lulea on the Gulf of Bothnia. It is one
of the world's two most northerly
railway stations.

INDIAN RAILWAYS

Of all world railways influenced by Britain, those of India best reflected the British presence. Railway development proceeded further in India than in any other part of Asia and by the 1950s 64,400 km (40,000 miles) were operating, comprising broad-gauge trunk lines, connecting large centres of population, and a network of narrow-gauge lines.

In the 19th century, four gauges emerged on the Indian subcontinent: 5 ft 6 in; metre; 2 ft 6 in; and 2 ft. The variety of companies operating these gauges had ordered a diversity of designs, which, with the exception of some metre-gauge standards , were largely unco-ordinated. The Central Provinces (from 1950 Madhya Pradesh), for example, had three railway systems.

● ENGINEERING STANDARDS COMMITTEES

This led the British Engineering Standards Committee (BESA) to appoint

● **LEFT**
The inside-cylinder 4-4-0 express-passenger hauling version of the inside-cylinder 0-6-0, again with an LNER aura – in this case the Manchester, Sheffield and Lincolnshire Railway's Pollitt 4-4-0s.

a subcommittee, composed of several leading British locomotive mechanical engineers, to prepare a set of standard designs for the subcontinent. In 1905, eight locomotive types were suggested to cover all broad-gauge requirements across India. The designs were classic British products: inside-cylinder 0-6-0s and 4-4-0s with common boilers, Atlantics, 4-6-0s and 2-8-0 heavy goods.

In 1924, the newly appointed Locomotive Standards Committee (LSC) was asked to make a new set of designs, in accordance with the need for more powerful locomotives. The committee presented eight basic types. The main ones were three Pacifics, XA, XB and XC, for branch-, medium- and heavy-passenger work; two Mikados, XD and XE, for medium and heavy goods respectively; and XT 0-4-2Ts for branch-line work.

Standard designs for metre and narrow gauge were also produced. Following the prefix X for the broad gauge came Y for metre gauge, Z for 2 ft 6 in gauge and Q for 2 ft gauge.

● AMERICAN INFLUENCE

A dramatic change occurred during World War II, Britain could not supply sufficient locomotives for India's increased traffic requirements and many new designs were ordered from North

● **LEFT**
A typically British 2-8-0 classified HSM from India's South Eastern Railway. These were once main-line heavy-freight haulers on the Bengal & Nagpur Railway. This last survivor is pictured on tripping duties in the Calcutta area.

- **LEFT**
An XC Class Pacific 4-6-2 of Indian Railways. These engines bear a striking resemblance to Gresley's Pacifics. Both types were introduced in the 1920s.

- **BELOW**
The heavy-freight hauling version of the XC was the XE 2-8-2. It bore a striking resemblance to Gresley's P1s of 1925.

- **BOTTOM**
One of Indian Railways's standard inside-cylinder 0-6-0s. These proliferated throughout many of the broad-gauge systems of the subcontinent. In common with the X types, these engines bear a striking resemblance to LNER classes, in this case the Pom Pom J11s of Great Central Railway (GCR).

America. These designs contrasted dramatically with the British engines and set a precedent for the remainder of steam development in India, because of suitability and popularity.

Three notable designs appeared on the 5 ft 6 in gauge: the AWC, which was an Indian version of Major Marsh's famous S160 of World War II; the class AWE, which was an Americanized version of the XE 2-8-2; and a lighter mixed-traffic Mikado 2-8-2 classified AWD/CWD. These three classes totalled 909 locomotives, 809 (89 per cent) of them being the light Mikado from mixed-traffic work. All entered service between 1943–9.

INDIAN XE CLASS 2-8-2	
Date	1930
Builder	William Beardmore Dalmuir, Vulcan Foundry, Lancashire, England
Client	East Indian Railway
Gauge	5 ft 6 in
Driving wheels	5 ft 1½ in
Capacity	Cylinders 23 x 30 in
Total weight	200 tons

CHINESE LOCOMOTIVE TRADITIONS

Railway development came late in China, and an incredible locomotive-building programme and standardization of types occurred in the years following World War II.

● EARLY DEVELOPMENT WITH FOREIGN LOANS

As recently as 1930, China had fewer than 16,000 km (10,000 miles) of railway. During the early years of the 20th century, China's railways were developed by a number of organizations, but

● LEFT
This streamlined Pacific classified SL7 is of a type built in Japan by Kawasaki and at the works of the South Manchurian Railway. These engines worked the high-speed Asia day-train between Dairen (the Japanese name for Dalian) and Mukden (modern Shenyang). The class was introduced in 1934.

invariably they turned to American imported locomotives of modest proportions. America's vigorous drive to promote the export of locomoties proved effective in China. The similarity in size between America and China, along with the varied terrain which the two countries

USATC S160 2-8-0	
Date	1943
Builders	American Locomotive Company (Alco); Baldwin Locomotive Company; Lima Locomotive Company
Client	United States Army Transportation Corps of Engineers (USATE)
Gauge	4 ft 8½ in
Driving wheels	4 ft 9 in
Capacity	2 cylinders 19 x 26 in
Total weight	125 tons

● LEFT
In the years following World War II, a number of Major Marsh's classic S160 2-8-0s were transferred to China in a programme to rebuild the country's railways.

● **RIGHT**
A China Railway's JF Class 2-8-2 Mikado on heavy shunt duties at Sankong Bridge, Haerbain (Harbin), the capital of Heilongjiang Province, north-eastern China.

had in common, rendered the American locomotive relatively easy to sell and well suited to the task in hand.

● **THE SOUTH MANCHURIAN RAILWAY**

The most developed part of China was Manchuria, and the South Manchurian Railway, although Japanese owned, was almost entirely American in its equipment and operation as a result of America having provided most of Japan's railway. In 1931, Japan took over Manchuria and with it the North Manchurian Railway. Locomotives operated in Manchuria were locally made as well as imported from Japan.

The advancement of railway and industrial operation in Manchuria led to

the South Manchurian Railway's introducing the streamlined "Asia" train in 1934, which operated a fast air-conditioned service between Dalian and Shenyang, or Makden as it was then known. Streamlined Pacific locomotives were built for this service both in Japan and South Manchuria.

● **RAILWAYS UNDER CHIANG KAI-SHEK**

Under the nationalist government of Chiang Kai-shek, development of railways was proceeding in other parts of the country in the 1930s. In 1937, the outbreak of the Sino-Japanese War ended new building. As this war went on, 80 per cent of China's railways were either destroyed or fell into Japanese hands.

● **RIGHT**
A China Railway's JF Class 2-8-2 Mikado on heavy shunt duties at Sankong Bridge, Haerbain (Harbin), the capital of Heilongjiang Province, north-eastern China.

● **RIGHT**
A former Soviet Union FD Class 2-10-2 engine, introduced in 1931. About 1,250 of these engines were transferred to China in the 1950s. The Chinese railway's standard QJ Class was derived from them. The FDs were themselves derived from an American design.

● **RIGHT**
Little British design influence permeated China's railways. American, Russian and indigenous factors were all the more prevalent. An exception is this Mogul, believed to be designed in Glasgow, Scotland, but built in China.

However, China's central government continued to build lines in the west, in areas not occupied by the Japanese.

● **KMT: RAILWAYS UNDER COMMUNISTS**

Japan's surrender in 1945 found China's railways in an appalling state. Aid came through the United Nations Relief and Rehabilitation Adminstration (UNRRA) scheme, which again brought huge numbers of American locomotives to Chinese soil. The ongoing Chinese Civil War caused further damage.

By the time of Mao's victory in 1949, the railways were in terrible disarray. Only half of the system was active. The following decades provided some stability under a powerful national identity and a centrally planned economy. The railways flowered under this regime. Herein lay the seeds of China's "Golden Age" of railways, expanding from the 1950s to the present day.

SOUTH-EAST ASIAN RAILWAYS

This section covers the railways of Peninsular Malaysia, from 1957 the successor-state to the British-controlled Federation of Malaya; of Thailand proper and Peninsular Thailand, which joins Peninsular Malaysia at the Kra Isthmus; of Indonesia, the Philippines and Taiwan.

● PENINSULAR MALAYSIA

In 1909 the last link of the line between two island cities of the then-British colony called the Straits Settlements, Penang and Singapore, respectively at the north and south ends of Peninsular Malaysia, was opened. Termini were on the mainland, at ferry ports serving the islands. The engines used on this line were the Pacifics, which, although small by British and continental standards, were robust machines weighing about 76 tons. With a 4-6-4 wheel arrangement, the locomotives had large headlights and cowcatchers.

In 1938, three-cylinder Pacific express-passenger locomotives were introduced on the Malayan metre-gauge line between Singapore, Kuala Lumpur,

capital of Perak State, and Prai, the railway terminus and seaport on the mainland, opposite George Town on Penang Island. Part of this line ascended the 1,000 m (3,300 ft) high Taiping Pass near Ipoh, the commercial centre of the Kinta Valley tin-mining region of Perak. These heavy gradients called for a special type of locomotive. The three-cylinder 4-6-2 Pacifics had a relatively small boiler but at high pressure provided the latent energy needed for developing a high tractive power.

The Pacifics were used on long runs but there were branch lines on which a tender-engine was unsuitable. For these, a 4-6-4 two-cylinder tank-engine was

● ABOVE
The Insular Lumber Company on the Philippine island of Negros operated the world's last four-cylinder compound 0-6-6-0 Mallet. It was built by Baldwin in the 1920s.

● ABOVE
One of South-east Asia's most remarkable systems is the stone railway at Gunung Kataren in northern Sumatra, Indonesia. The line conveys stones from a riverbed to a crushing plant for use as track ballast. Built to 60 cm gauge, this veteran came from Orenstein & Koppel in 1920.

● LEFT
Three standard Japanese 3 ft 6 in gauge designs working in Taiwan. Left, a Taiwan Government Railway Class DT595 2-8-0 (Japanese National Railway 9600 Class); centre, a Class CT192 Mogul (JNR Class 8620); right, a Class DT673 Mikado (JNR Class D51) – 1,100 of these mixed-traffic 2-8-2s were built between 1936–45.

● RIGHT
A 4-6-0 built for metre-gauge Royal Siamese
State Railways in 1919 by North British of
Glasgow, Scotland.

● RIGHT
A 4-6-0 built for metre-gauge Royal Siamese
State Railways in 1919 by North British of
Glasgow, Scotland.

4 - 6 - 0	
Date	1919
Builder	North British Glasgow, Scotland
Client	Royal Siamese State Railways
Gauge	Metre
Driving wheels	4 ft
Capacity	Cylinders 14½ x 22 in

used. It was fitted with cowcatchers at
both ends so that it was suitable for
running in both directions. Like the
Pacifics, these 4-6-4Ts were fitted with
Caprotti valve gear.

● THAILAND
In Siam (Muang-Thai to Thais and
since 1949 Thailand), in the rice-
growing and jungle country, the metre-
gauge railway was laid with relatively

light rails on a soft road bed. Powerful
locomotives were needed, and in
1925 26 Pacific 2-8-2s were bought from
the USA. They were woodfired,
and routes were arranged so that the
engines would travel out and back to
their home station on one tenderful
of fuel. The round trips were
193–225 km (120–140 miles) long.
This arrangement meant frequent
engine changes *en route*.

● ABOVE
A battered, hybridized, American-built
Mikado, believed to have been constructed
by Alco in 1921, at work on the metals of
the Ma Ao Sugar Central railway on the
Philippine island of Negros. These
locomotives draw freshly cut sugar cane
from the fields to the mills.

● RIGHT
A Thai railways metre-gauge Pacific 4-6-2, No.
823, which, with the MacArthur 2-8-2s, was
one of Thailand's last steam locomotives.

AUSTRALASIAN RAILWAYS

New South Wales (NSW) entered the 20th century with a scheme to have main-line traffic handled by standard classes for passenger services, the P6 (later C32) Class 4-6-0; for goods traffic, the 1524 (later D50 Class) 2-8-0, of which 280 were built; and for suburban working the S636 (later C30) Class, numbering 145 units.

● NEW SOUTH WALES

In the mid-1920s, as traffic grew, 75 C36 Class units took over major passenger services. From 1929, 25 4-8-2 D57 Class units were introduced for heavyfreight. With extreme traffic during World War II, 30 new C38 Class Pacifics were built, becoming the foremost express-locomotive. With the need for new goods locomotives after the war, 42 4-8-4+4-8-4 Garratts were obtained to carry the brunt of the load prior to the arrival of diesels.

● TASMANIA

Tasmania also used Garratts – the 2 ft gauge K Class of 1910 being the first Garratt in the world. The 3 ft 6 in lines followed, with the L Class 2-6-2+2-6-2 for goods traffic and the M Class 4-4-2+2-4-4s for passenger traffic.

● SOUTH AUSTRALIA

In South Australia, ten 4-6-2 passenger, ten 2-8-2 goods and ten 4-8-2 mixed-traffic locomotives entered service in 1926. These were of American design but built in England. On the narrow gauge, the T Class were the mainstay of the traffic, almost to the end of steam.

● WESTERN AUSTRALIA

Western Australia introduced 57 F Class 4-8-0s in 1902. These were accompanied by 65 E Class 4-6-2s for passenger services. Larger Pacifics entered service

from 1924 onwards. Following World War II, the fleet was augmented by 60 light-line Beyer Peacock 4-8-2 W Class and 25 heavy 2-8-2 V Class from Robert Stephenson & Hawthorn.

● AUSTRALIAN NETWORK AND THE TCR

The development of Australia's railway network was complicated but striking. The gauge was not uniform (New South Wales was mostly the standard 4 ft 8½ in, South Australia mostly broad 5 ft 3 in gauge and all Queensland was narrow 3 ft

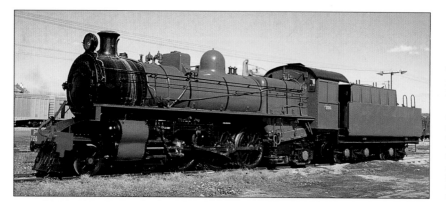

● RIGHT
The pride of
Australia's NSW
Railways, No. 3801,
introduced in 1943,
waiting to depart
with an air-
conditioned
passenger-train
in 1963.

SAR RX 4-6-0	
Date	1909
Builder	SAR Islington/NBLC Walker (SA)
Client	NSWGR
Gauge	4 ft 8½ in
Wheels	5 ft 9 in
Capacity	Cylinders 18 x 24 in
Weight	201 tons

● RIGHT
In 1899, South
Australian Railways
(SAR) started
converting 30 R
Class 4-6-0
locomotives to Rx
Class by providing
higher-pressure
boilers. An
additional 54 were
newly built in 1909.
This example,
RX93, is pictured at
the Mile End depot
in 1965.

written off in 1957. The Pacific was
further developed, eventually to the Ab
class of 1915, of which 141 were built,
and to a tank-engine, the Wab class. The
Ab Class is claimed to be the first
locomotive in the world to have been
capable of 1 hp for each 100 lb of weight.

Tank engines played a major part on
the lines of this small nation, the 4-6-4T
W Class of 50 units being one of the
more prolific. Garratts were also tried in
1928 but failed, due less to design faults
than to the light drawgear on New
Zealand rolling stock and the short
crossing loops, making economical
running almost impossible. Heavier
conventional locomotives followed.

6 in gauge). Of the continent's some
45,000 km (28,000 miles) of railway, all
but about 3 per cent, 1,290 km
(800 miles), was state-owned by the
1950s. Of that length, 1,694 km (1,052
miles) were occupied by the
Transcontinental (East-West) Railway
completed in 1917. The TCR crosses
South Australia and Western Australia,
linking Port Augusta, at the head of the
Spencer Gulf, and Perth with its port of
Fremantle on the Indian Ocean. It
crosses the Great Victoria Desert and the
Nullarbar Plain, serves the goldfields of
Kalgoorlie and the agricultural industry,
and runs link lines to Port Pirie and to
Alice Springs in the Northern Territory.

● NEW ZEALAND
New Zealand's main claim to fame is the
development of the world's first true
Pacific locomotive, 13 of which were
supplied by Baldwin in 1901. These
engines had a long life, the last being

● BELOW
Designed for traffic on light lines, this
example of a J Class was one of 40 delivered to
New Zealand at the start of World War II. A
modified Ja Class supplied in 1946 is in front.
The two locomotives are pictured at Fielding-
Marton in 1972.

AFRICAN RAILWAYS

The years before the start of World War I were exciting and dynamic on South Africa's railways, many designs being produced. The 20th century brought a foretaste of the giants to come, powerful 2-8-2s, 4-8-0s and 4-8-2s being put into traffic with some racy Pacific designs.

● **UNION OF SOUTH AFRICA**
The immense distances and sparsely populated country called for strong locomotives, many of which had four-wheeled leading bogies to cope with cheaply laid track beds.

South African Railways (SAR) were formed in 1910 by the amalgamation of Africa's main railway companies. These were the Cape Government Railway (CGR), the Natal Government Railway (NGR) and the Central South African Railway (CSAR).

The country's first articulated locomotives were 2-6-6-0 compounds built by the American Locomotive Company (Alco). The type was introduced on to Natal's heavily graded, sharply curved routes.

Just as the giant Mallet conquered

● **BELOW**
Garratts on the Greytown Line in Natal, South Africa. One of SAR's pugnacious GMA Class 4-8-2+2-8-4 Garratts prepares to leave New Hanover, Natal, with full freight for Greytown. These powerful secondary Garratts, descended from the GM Class of 1938, climbed 1:40 gradients with only 60 lb weight.

● **ABOVE**
In contrast with the typical four- and six-coupled tanks of British industry, South Africa's engines were fully fledged mainliners to haul trains over undulating tracks to SAR connections often many miles from collieries. This North British-built 4-8-2T is one of a standard class exported from Glasgow, Scotland, to South Africa for industrial use.

● **LEFT**
SAR 3 ft 6 in-gauge 4-8-2s of the 1930s.

America, so the Garratt articulated conquered Africa. South Africa's railways were one of the largest users of Garratts from their introduction to the country in 1920. They quickly proved themselves superior to the Mallet on a network that ran through difficult terrain abounding in heavy gradients and curves with relatively lightly laid track.

The Garratt's boiler and firebox are free of axles and so can be built to whatever size is needed. A deep firebox allowed for ample generation of steam and full combustion of gases. By placing the engine's wheels and cylinders under a front water unit and with the rear coal units situated either side of the boiler, the engine's weight is spread over a wide area. With the front and rear units articulated from the boiler, a large, powerful locomotive can be built capable of moving heavy loads over curved gradients and

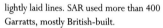

SAR "BIG BILL" 4-8-2	
Date	1925
Builder	Baldwin, American Locomotive Company (USA), Breda (Milan, Italy), North British (Glasgow, Scotland)
Client	South African Railways (SAR)
Gauge	3 ft 6 in
Wheels	5 ft
Capacity	Cylinders 24 x 28 in
Weight	173 tons

● **FAR LEFT**
The SAR Class 15CA, 4-8-2 "Big Bills" were the first large American engines imported to South Africa. They had a profound influence on locomotive development. This Italian-built example is seen leaving Panpoort, Transvaal.

● **NAMIBIA (FORMERLY SOUTH WEST AFRICA)**

In the years following World War II, 100 2-8-4 Berkshires were put into operation for branch-line work, particularly over the 45 lb rail lines in South West Africa (Namibia since independence in 1990). They had cylindrical bogie tenders for long-range operation in waterless areas. The type displaced the ageing Class 7 and Class 8 4-8-0s of half a century earlier.

lightly laid lines. SAR used more than 400 Garratts, mostly British-built.

The 1920s also saw the introduction of large 4-8-2s and Pacifics of pure American construction. These set the precepts for the giants that followed, such as the 15F Class and 23 Class 4-8-2s. These formed the mainstay of steam motive power from the 1930s until the end of steam operations.

● **ABOVE RIGHT**
The Mallett was little used in South Africa but this 2-6-6-2, four-cylinder compound Class MH was one of five built by North British in 1915. At their introduction, they were the largest locomotives in the world on 3 ft 6 in gauge track.

● **RIGHT**
A South African Railways (SAR) Class 23 4-8-2 heads northwards from Bloemfontein, capital of Orange Free State. These American-inspired engines of 3 ft 6 in gauge were constructed in the late 1930s by both British and German builders and totalled 136 examples.

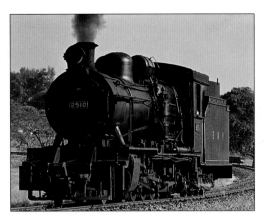

● **LEFT**
A former
Tanganyika Railway
ML Class 2-8-2,
complete with Geisl
ejector and air
brakes – and one of
Tanganyika
Railway's last
designs.

● **OPPOSITE
TOP LEFT**
The plate from a
locomotive built for
Rhodesian Railways
by Beyer Peacock of
Manchester,
England.

● **ZIMBABWE**

Railways were essential to the rich
development potential of landlocked
Zimbabwe (Southern Rhodesia until
1964, Rhodesia 1964–78). Routes
extended to the Indian Ocean ports, eastwards to Beira in Mozambique, southwards through South Africa to Durban in
Natal. A third route was opened up northwards, across the Victoria Falls at Hwange
(until 1982 Wankie) and on through the
copper belt. This route reached the
Atlantic Ocean ports via the Bengeula
Railway in Angola. By 1920, when
Rhodesia Railways (RR) was formed, a
unified 3 ft 6 in gauge was in operation.

Motive power was not dissimilar from
that of South Africa, with 4-8-0s and 4-
8-2 Mountains. As the national wealth of
this vast region was developed, however,
the demand for heavier trains became

huge and articulated locomotives vital.
After a Kitson-Mayer phase, the Garratt
phase was introduced to standardize the
system. Almost half the locomotives built
for Rhodesian Railways were British-built
Garratts, embracing all duties from
branch-line work, through heavy freights
to expresses with the racy 15th Class
4-6-4+4-6-4s. These handled mixed-
traffic duties and reached speeds of
70 mph with passenger-trains.

● **EAST AFRICA**

In East Africa, the British-built Kenyan
and Ugandan lines and the German-built

● **LEFT**
Following the lead
by the USA the wide
firebox appeared
early on Britain's
locomotive exports,
especially those
bound for African
countries. A typical
example was the
Rhodesian Railways
12A Class 4-8-2. The
example shown is
No. 190, built in
1926 by North
British, Glasgow,
Scotland.

● **RIGHT**
A former Rhodesian
Railways 16th Class
Garratt 2-8-2+2-8-2,
built by Beyer
Peacock of
Manchester,
England, in 1929,
working at the
Transvaal
Navigation Colliery,
South Africa.

A typical African plantation-train during the early 20th century at Lugazi, Uganda. The unidentified engine, with ornate spark-arresting chimney, is of European origin.

railways of neighbouring Tanzania (formerly Tanganyika) were metre gauge. The Ugandan railway in its early years used early Indian metre-gauge types, notably E Class 0-4-2s and the celebrated F Class 0-6-0s. Invariably, motive power

CLASS 54 2-8-2+2-8-2 GARRATT	
Date	1944
Builder	Beyer Peacock, Manchester, England
Client	Kenya & Ugandan Railway (via UK Ministry of Supply)
Gauge	Metre
Wheels	3 ft 9½ in
Capacity	4 cylinders 19 x 24 in
Weight	185 tons

blossomed and embraced a Mallet stage and some Garratts, although the 4-8-0 was adopted as a general standard, many examples being to Indian BESA designs.

By the time the Kenya & Ugandan Railway (KUR) was formed in 1926, extremely powerful 2-8-2s worked the line linking the Kenyan Indian Ocean port of Mombasa and the Kenyan capital at Nairobi. The network also had a wide variety of Garratts, although these remained in a minority compared with the conventional locomotives, many of which were used on lighter sections of this vast area of Africa.

● ANGOLA
The 1,347 km (837 mile) long Angola Railway (Benguela Railway) was built by the Portuguese to link their then west and east coast possessions in southern Africa, respectively Angola and Mozambique. From the west, it runs from the Atlantic Ocean ports of Lobito and Benguela, to the Democratic Republic of Congo (formerly Zaire),

linking to Port Francqui (Ilebo), the Copper Belt of Zambia (formerly Northern Rhodesia) and Zimbabwe, and on to the Indian Ocean ports of Sofala (formerly Beira) and Maputo (Lourenço Marques until 1975) in Mozambique, and Durban, then on to the Cape.

It achieved world renown for the eucalyptus-burning Garratts, which worked over one of the sections climbing the steep coastal escarpment inland from the Atlantic. These red-liveried mammoths shot columns of fire into the sky at night and were regarded by some as one of the railway sights of the world.

NORTHERN AFRICAN RAILWAYS

Railway development in Africa was essential to open up the industrial potential of the continent's interior and provide vital lifelines for the movement of materials. Africa has benefited vastly from her railways but their piecemeal, often parochial, building defied the obvious ideal of a Pan-African system. Had the railways been built with this vision, Africa would be an infinitely more prosperous continent than she is today.

● ALGERIA

Algeria's railways were built and engineered by the French from the mid-19th century. A large network of lines of various types emerged, including through links with neighbouring Tunisia and Morocco. The standard gauge, fed by metre-gauge lines, saw many 0-6-0s. Moguls and standard De Glehn compounds of types commonly seen in Europe.

In the 1920s, 2-10-0s appeared for hauling heavy mineral trains. Famous types working in Algeria included some Prussian G8s and three-cylinder G12s. Most celebrated, however, were the Algerian Garratts. These, built in France in 1932, were the most powerful express-passenger-locomotives ever to

● **LEFT**
Nameplates from former Gold Coast Railway's steam locomotives commemorating British governors, tribes and slaving forts.

EGYPTIAN STATE RAILWAYS (ESR) ATLANTIC 4-4-2	
Date	1906
Builder	North British, Glasgow, Scotland
Client	Egyptian State Railways (ESR)
Gauge	4 ft 8½ in
Driving wheels	6 ft 3 in
Capacity	Cylinders 17 x 26 in

● **BELOW**
These British-styled Atlantics were delivered to ESR in 1906 from the North British Works in Glasgow, Scotland, for operation on Egypt's standard-gauge network.

operate outside the USA.

By the 1950s, a rail network of more than 4,800 km (3,000 miles) penetrated all parts of Algeria. Two lines stretched into the Sahara to link with motor routes stretching to then French West Africa.

● TUNISIA

Tunisia had both standard- and metre-gauge lines, although no standard-gauge locomotives were delivered into the country after 1928. During World War II, American S160 2-8-0s, British Hunslet Austerity 0-6-0STs and some British Great Western Dean goods were all introduced for military operations.

● MOROCCO

Morocco's railways were also French-dominated, the country having become a French protectorate in 1912. Through-services were run between Marrakech in

established. Sudan has a great will to
operate a good, viable railway system.
Additions to the network were being
made as late as 1960.

Pacifics and Mikados, many with light
axle loadings, were a mainstay of Sudan's
motive power. Sudan also operated
4-6-4 + 4-6-4 Garratts pulling 1,600 ton
trains between Atbara, Khartoum and
Wad Medani. In contrast, English-
looking 0-6-0Ts handled shunting and
local tripping work. The last of these was
not built until 1951, notwithstanding
Sudan received diesel-shunters as early
as 1936.

The pièce de résistance of
conventional Sudanese motive power
came with the 42 500 Class 4-8-2s
delivered by North British, of Glasgow,
Scotland, in 1954.

the west and Tunisia in the east, a
distance of 2,400 km (1,491 miles).

● EGYPT

The Egyptian State Railway (ESR) is the
oldest in Africa and blossomed following
British occupation of the Nile Valley in
1882. The railway was built and run by
the British. Though the ESR operated a
vast diversity of types, British operating
methods and many British designs were
in evidence. Much of Egypt's express-
passenger work was handled by the
Atlantic 4-4-2s, backed by either 0-6-0s
or Moguls for mixed-traffic work.

World War II's North African
Campaign demanded movement of really
heavy freight trains. Many British Stanier
8F 2-8-0s were sent, of which 60 were
adopted by the ESR after the war.

Egypt's rich locomotive tradition
ended with a class of oil-burning, French-
built Pacifics delivered as late as 1955.

● SUDAN

Egypt's standard-gauge lines contrast
with the 3 ft 6 in gauge network of
neighbouring Sudan where railway
building proper began around the turn of
the century. One of the earliest systems
ran from the Nile Valley to the Red Sea
then southwards through the capital,
Khartoum. Although much of this early
railway building had a military purpose,
the beginnings of a national railway were

● ABOVE
The spinning driving wheels of a Class 500
4-8-2 of Sudan Railway.

● BELOW
A mixed train on Sudan State Railways headed
by a standard oilburning Mikado 2-8-2 built
by North British, of Glasgow, Scotland.

● WEST AFRICA

In West Africa, Britain, France and
Germany all introduced railways to their
colonial possessions.

SOUTH AMERICAN RAILWAYS

South America's railways are of great diversity, reflecting the vast geographical contrasts of a continent that ranges from the tropical rain forests of the Amazon, to the passes of the Andes standing at 4,266 m (14,000 ft), through to the verdant beef-rearing flatlands of the Argentine pampas.

● ARGENTINA

Argentina had by far the greatest density of railways, with over 100 different types of locomotive operating over five different gauges. The British-owned railways of Argentina constituted the largest commercial enterprise ever to operate outside an investing nation. With many of the country's railway systems operated by Britain, Argentina was a huge recipient of British products. British-built steam locomotives fired on Welsh coal gave Argentina one of the world's most successful economies, exporting vast tonnages of meat, grain and fruit.

● URUGUAY

The railways of neighbouring Uruguay were also British-owned. Beyer Peacock of Manchester, England, was a principal

builder over many years. Manchester was connected with the vast Fray Bentos meat corporation based on Fray Bentos town in Uruguay.

● BRAZIL

The vastness of Brazil, with its network of 5 ft 3 in and metre-gauge lines and a huge diversity of secondary routes, plantation and industrial railways, also ensured an incredibly rich locomotive heritage. American-built locomotives predominated with British classics on the metre-gauge Leopoldina system.

● PARAGUAY

Neighbouring Paraguay's standard-gauge main-line railway linked the capital and chief port, Asunción, with Encarnación

● LEFT
Mixed freight to Fray Bentos, in Uruguay. The Uruguayan Railway's last-surviving T Class 2-8-0 named Ing Pedro Magnou is heading a train bound for the meat-canning port on the Uruguay River. This 2-8-0 has a distinctive Scottish Highland Railway aura about it.

A 5 ft 6 in gauge survivor of the Chilean Railway's 38 Class on pilot duties at San Bernardo works, outside Santiago in Chile. It is probably the last survivor from Roger's of New Jersey, USA, having come from those works in 1896.

386 km (240 miles) away on the Argentine border. This railway was also British-owned and operated. The main motive power for much of the present century has been provided by woodburning Edwardian Moguls, exported from the North British Works in Glasgow, Scotland.

● BOLIVIA AND CHILE

The railways of Bolivia, South America's other landlocked nation, connected Chile, over the Andes to the west, with Brazil and Argentina, over the humid lowlands to the east. The country's locomotive heritage was diverse, with a rich mixture of European, American and British schools of design.

● TRANS-ANDEAN
RAILWAY (TAR)

The Trans-Andean Railway (TAR) completed in 1910 links Valparaiso, Chile's greatest seaport, with Buenos Aires, the Argentine capital, crossing the Andes and desolate Patagonia at the Uspallata Pass between Mendoza in Argentina and Santiago in Chile. The near 3 km (2 mile) long Trans-Andean RR tunnel crosses at the pass's highest point, at 3,986 m (13,082 ft), near the Western Hemisphere's highest peak, 6,958 m (22,835 ft) high Mount Aconcagua. The link cut the 11-day

BUENOS AIRES & GREAT SOUTHERN 11B CLASS 2-8-0	
Date	1914
Builder	Beyer Peacock, North British and Vulcan Foundry
Client	Buenos Aires & Great Southern Railway (BAGS)
Gauge	5 ft 6 in
Driving wheels	4 ft 7½ in
Capacity	Cylinders 19 x 26 in
Total weight	105 tons

The last surviving Kitson-Meyer 0-6-6-0 – known as "The Dodo of the Atacama" – at work in Chile's Atacama Desert. These locomotives once brought gold and nitrates to Pacific coast ports.

journey by boat via the Magellan Strait to 40 hours overland. The line climbs hills so steep that part of it uses cog-wheel apparatus.

● COLOMBIA, ECUADOR
AND PERU

Colombia, Ecuador and Chile drew their locomotive traditions mainly from American builders. Peru had a mixture of American and British designs.

There were no locomotive-building traditions in South America or Africa. Both these continents were entirely dependent on the building traditions developed in Britain, Europe and America.

A woodburning Edwardian Mogul from North British, of Glasgow, Scotland, heads along the standard-gauge main line from the Paraguayan capital Asunción to Encarnación on the Argentine border. This railway is the last all-steam worked international main line in the world.

A 2-8-2, No. 183, of Guatemalan Railways, at Gualán in 1971.

INDEX

CONVERSION CHART

To convert:	Multiply by:
Inches to centimetres	2.54
Centimetres to inches	0.3937
Millimetres to inches	0.03937
Feet to metres	0.3048
Metres to feet	3.281
Miles to kilometres	1.609
Kilometres to miles	0.6214
Tons to tonnes	1.016
Tonnes to tons	0.9842

NOTES

NOTES

NOTES

NOTES